Tails of Birding

RANDOM ESSAYS INSPIRED BY BIRDS AND BIRDWATCHING

CHRIS PETRAK

Revised Edition, 2019

PONDVILLE PRESS
SOUTH NEWFANE, VT & PHILADELPHIA

Petrak, Chris, date
Tails of birding, random essays inspired by birds and birdwatching;
photographs by Chris Petrak
Includes bibliographical references
ISBN-13: 978-1461066316
1. Birds - Vermont - Anecdotes.
2. Birdwatching - Vermont - Anecdotes.
3. Nature - Observations - Reflections

For Julius, Adam, Celia, Oliver, Zachary
in the hope that you will always love and respect
the natural world

and for

"2"

Contents

Prologue

In 1997, I retired as the head of staff of a downtown church in an eastern Pennsylvania town and moved to Vermont. One of my goals for this very early retirement was to spend more time birding, a hobby which I enjoyed, but at which I was, I now know, only marginally adept.

I grew up in Detroit where bird life was limited, and nature was distant and esoteric. With the help of Scouting, and summers working at a camp in Northern Michigan, I became comfortable in the out-of-doors. I enjoyed the "big picture," but never had the time, or took the time, to become familiar with the "details."

That began to change in 1979 when my spouse finally got me to sit down on the deck of the tiny country home we had built in western Pennsylvania, and be still. I began to notice the birds. During the 1980s when we visited family in Cape May, New Jersey, and when we took long family trips "out west," the binoculars went everywhere, and my interest in birds and birding began to grow. I checked off a lot of birds, had fun, worked very hard to learn bird songs, started to develop some skills, and developed a confidence that I was a good birder. The confidence was probably greater than the fact.

During that first summer in Vermont, we (the plural of the pronoun being my favorite companion and spouse of many years) spent the weekdays working on our old village house, and the weekends going to concerts, fairs, and community gatherings, and in general, discovering that we had found a very comfortable new home.

One of those weekends, we visited the homes of neighbors on the Rock River Artists Open Studio Tour. One "studio" was just around the corner, a lean-to shed where our potter neighbor fired his raku pots in old fifty gallon drums; he had a more conventional barn studio where he threw his pots and otherwise did what potters do. When we visited, a dozen people had just left, and we had time to talk. Conversation went to birds and he invited me to join him the next morning to go see the nest of a Northern Goshawk.

We drove into the heights of Marlboro, visited briefly with one of his many artist friends, then began walking an abandoned road into the forest. At a brushy intersection of old roads, he paused, he cocked his head, then began pishing. ("Pish, pish, pish" - or variations of the sound, is used by birders to lure a curious bird into the open.) Three different wood warblers came out of the thick foliage or down from high branches to investigate.

A short distance further on, the abandoned track entered mature forest. Soon we heard, "ca-ca-ca-ca-ca." Then from a different angle, "ca-ca-ca-ca-ca."

He paused, listened, then whispered, "The young are calling. Let's try to get them to come closer." He began an exact imitation of what we had just heard: "ca-ca-ca-ca-ca." In moments we saw two birds flying from tree to tree, echoing one another and the human imitator. The young birds paused on a branch and we studied them through binoculars.

After a couple of minutes, he said, "Let's get out of here before the parents come back. You don't want to face an aggressive goshawk."

That was the beginning of my local birding in Vermont. It was also the first of many lessons I have learned from skilled Vermont birders.

The first December in Vermont I joined a team for the Brattleboro

Area Christmas Bird Count. Then I accompanied our local Audubon for a February trip to Plum Island on the Massachuset coast where I counted five new species: Snow Bunting, Glaucous Gull, White-winged Scoter, Northern Shrike, and at the very end of the day, Snowy Owl. I was off and running.

Sometime in 1999, I began contributing to "Tailfeathers" in the Brattleboro Reformer. Other contributors gradually dropped out and by the spring of 2000, I was the only person writing the column. Initially I narrated bird watching experiences and my birding hobby. But that could not sustain a weekly column. I began to weave in bird biology, science, bird history, book reviews, and whatever else pricked my interest. I expanded my library by adding out-of-print classics (Audubon, Bent, Forbush) and new publications by today's best birders and bird authors (Sibley, Kaufman, Dunne, and others).

My academic career began as a chemistry major, but soon changed to history where I could indulge my bent for research without the noxious odors of the laboratory. Eventually my profession became theology, but I continued my avocational interest in Imperial Rome and Byzantium; on several occasions I have turned my research interest to the writing of local history.

As brief as my early involvement in science was, I have maintained an interest in science, and a concern for the integrity of scientific research. As I have written about birds, I have done my very best to get the science right, but I emphasize that birding is a hobby. The great benefit of writing a weekly column about birds is how much I have had to learn in order to write. It also provides good excuse to buy books, go on birding trips, and chase birds around New England. There is always the Wednesday deadline.

For several years, I have had readers of my weekly column urge me to put them in book form. More recently, some followers of my blog have also begun the book query.

So here we are - a random collection of essays on birds and bird watching - random, because that is so often how the birds are encountered - in unplanned and unexpected ways.

∗ ∗ ∗

Most of the essays, and most of my birding, is done around my home in southeastern Vermont. Southeastern Vermont is Windham County, population about 35,000. It is mostly rural and small town; there are still a few working farms, but through most of the county, the forest has, or is, returning. The County is bordered to the east by the Connecticut River (elevation about 500 ft), and to the west by the spine of the Green Mountains, peaking at around 3,000 feet in elevation, and the site of several well-known ski areas. Most of the county consists of rounded, but often rugged hills, drained by clean mountain streams. In general this is the place to which many neo-tropical species come to breed.

The population and commercial center is Brattleboro, an old industrial town that is still a center for forest products, but now is also a center for the arts, strolling heifers in June, organic and green-economy entrepreneurs, and winter sports.

A few miles to the northeast of the confluence in Brattleboro of the West River with the Connecticut River, is the Rock River. Upstream is the small village of South Newfane where my old village/farm house sits on about a half acre along the river and adjoins hundreds of acres of regenerating forest, interspersed with old valley and hill farms and new residences.

The Brattleboro Retreat, an old and always progressive mental health facility, is located in Brattleboro. Years ago a working farm was a part of the Retreat; it included "meadows" for pasture. In the 1930s, a hydroelectric dam was built in Vernon a few miles down river on the

Connecticut. The dam flooded the meadows, creating a shallow lake that is used by canoers and kayakers when the waters are open, and by fishermen in all seasons. The old pasture is still known to locals as the "Retreat meadows." It is a great birding site.

The Vernon dam also created wetland habitat across the river in Hinsdale, often referred to as the Hinsdale setbacks.

A similar wetlands to the Retreat meadows is Herrick's Cove located at the confluence of the Connecticut and Williams Rivers 25 miles north of Brattleboro, and about five miles north of the hydroelectric dam in Bellows Falls. It is designated as an "Important Bird Area" and is a regular place of pilgrimage for bird watchers.

A ridge runs between the Connecticut and West River Valleys. Part of the ridge is known as Putney Mountain. A half mile walk through forest along the ridge line will bring one to a clearing where the Putney Mountain Hawk Watch counts migrating hawks during September and October. Manned entirely by volunteers, it is the only full time hawk watch site in Vermont.

You will encounter these places in the essays that follow, as well as more far flung places which attract birds and birders.

* * *

Often in these essays, I draw on the observations and research of others. I have avoided the use of footnotes, but I do reference sources and quotations in the "Chapter Notes." Please refer to those notes, and "Selected Resources" for more background and information. These have been my invaluable aids as I try to get the science and facts right.

* * *

Vermont is a small state, and a very rural state. One's close neighbors are the people in the town (or township as it would be known in many places - a roughly six mile square). Drive a hundred miles north to a birding hotspot (like Dead Creek Wildlife Management area for migrating Snow Geese, or the Lake Champlain Islands), and you are likely to meet someone you know. The birding community is a community of good neighbors, who are, in fact, neighbors, though they may live across the state. They share interest, concerns, and life style.

So ... in making this book possible, I begin by thanking the Vermont community, and the birders in Vermont. Thank you to the scientists whose friendship and presence makes me work at getting the science right. Thank you to the superb birders from whom I have learned much about birding. Thank you to that quirky group of hawk watchers who keep the slow times on the mountain always interesting. Thank you to the bright and interesting members of the board of our local Audubon chapter who never let business get in the way of good conversation and bird gossip. Most importantly, thank you to my favorite companion and spouse of many years.

Good birding!

Chris Petrak
South Newfane, Vermont
April, 2011

Grout Pond Campground

CHAPTER 1

THE START OF A BIG DAY

The first notes of the robin's song told me that it was nearly morning. Even so, I did not push my head out from beneath the covers to confirm what my ears were telling me. I stayed buried in my sleeping bag, curled tight against the chill air.

The sweet whistled notes of the White-throated Sparrow joined the robin's warble: "pooor, sam ... peabody, peabody, peabody." I stirred and turned in my sleeping bag. Tentatively I looked out; the night sky was beginning to grow lighter. I lay still, listening as the thin chipping song of a distant Dark-eyed Junco joined in. I began stretching limbs from the night's rest. Another songster limbered his vocal chords, the clear, flute-like song rising up the scale.

There was no movement from the nearby bundled lump wrapped in a sleeping bag. Nevertheless, I said, "Do you hear the Swainson's Thrush?"

"Yea ... nice way to start a day."

"There's a junco singing."

"I hear it."

"Ready to start the day?"

"No use wasting it in here."

Outside of the cocoon of the sleeping bag, I dressed quickly, rolled my bed and emerged from the tent. The cloudless sky was golden from the sun which had yet to breach the horizon. There was a thin coating of frost on the windshield of the truck. From several directions, Magnolia Warblers sang in the spruce trees: "weeta, weeta, weet-tee-oh."

It was Tuesday morning, about 4:45, and three of us were beginning our annual "Big Day" when we would travel around Windham County in an effort to identify as many species of birds as possible in one day. In previous years we had skipped the higher elevations of Somerset and Stratton. This year we decided that we could include them if we camped out, so we spent the night in the Forest Service campground at Grout Pond.

The day had actually begun a couple of hours earlier when four Barred Owls talked back and forth with one another. But now it was dawn and the birds were awakening, anxious to begin their territorial singing, mate acquisition, and nest building. It is a short season for breeding - shorter yet on the mountain ridges - and they were quickly about their task.

And so were we - anxious to be about our self-imposed task of hearing and seeing the birds. We gulped juice, downed a banana in a couple of bites, then headed down the mile long trail toward the northernmost finger of Somerset Reservoir. But you could hardly call our pace a rapid one; there was too much to listen to, too much flitting through the tree tops.

High overhead we heard the thin, wiry song of a Blackburnian Warbler. If you were to see just the back of this bird, you would be unimpressed - black, with a patch or stripe of white here and there. We picked up its movement through still unleafed tree tops. Binoculars focused, followed it to the end of a branch where it paused, lifted its head, and sang. It turned toward the east, and it seemed as though its throat suddenly burst into a flame-orange from the suns rays. But the sun's rays had yet to reach the tree tops. The flame illuminating the Blackburnian's throat came only from the plumage of the bird itself.

Woodland songbirds sang everywhere: Blue-headed and Red-eyed Vireos, Ovenbird, Northern Parula, Black-throated Blue and Black-throated Green Warblers, Red-breasted and White-breasted Nuthatches. Distantly a Pileated Woodpecker drummed; nearby a Yellow-bellied Sapsucker also drummed, but with a lighter touch, one which slowed down as though it were running out of energy. We watched a pair of Hairy Woodpeckers going in and out of a nest hole carrying food for their young.

When we reached Somerset Reservoir, the sun was just touching the tops of the surrounding hills. Mist rose off of the still water, its mirror-like surface barely disturbed by the languorous motion of a Common Merganser. A beaver slipped into the water, his head cutting through the calm surface like a propelled log until he broke the calm by slapping his tail.

Turning toward the thin tip of the reservoir, a large bird appeared. An adult Bald Eagle flapped upward, his powerful wings needing no assistance from warm thermals to gain altitude. Then from a nearby snag, a one year old eagle took flight.

In a dense shrub, a small brown bird moved furtively. Thinking it might be one of the uncommon, shy sparrows that nest much to the north, we searched carefully through the thicket. It was a Song

Sparrow; this normally curious, vociferous, conspicuous sparrow was building a nest. For the protection of its young-to-be, it was being as secretive as possible.

About seven o'clock we were back at our campsite, scarfing cereal, brewing coffee, and packing up. The campground host came by with his coffee mug and joined into our friendly banter, curious also about our day's activity.

"You do this sort of thing often?" he asked.

"Three or four times a year we spend the day together birding."

As he looked over our ragged, somewhat eccentric group, I was expecting him to say something like, "That's probably all you could stand of one another."

Instead, someone said, "I hear a raven." Talk ceased and binoculars went in the direction of the croaks. "It's chasing an eagle!" Moments later, an adult Bald Eagle flew low and majestically overhead - a different adult from the one seen earlier. This one was missing a primary feather.

Packed and fed, we were on the road. We had ticked forty species. It was 7:30 am. Already it was a day of Good Birding!

Fledgling Blue Jay

CHAPTER 2
JULY

In July, the best entertainment is free and available daily from my back porch. I can sit with an open book, but the words go unread and the pages unturned. This is the time when the resident nesting birds bring their broods around. I'd like to say that they are introducing the children, but they don't have much time for parental posturing over their handsome offspring. They are much too busy trying to satisfy the food demands of their adolescents.

Early in the season, when one bird feeds another bird, it is probably part of the courtship ritual of the species. Now it is parents and young. Occasionally the feeding is a quiet affair, a simple passing of food from one beak to the other. It is more likely to be a noisy, frantic, energetic affair, with the fledgling chipping and squawking, wings constantly aflutter, maw agape.

Again, early in the season, when one bird chases another, it is sex which drives the activity. Now when one bird chases another it is a young bird after its parent; the juvenile is unsatisfied with the food its parent has thrust down its gullet, and is demanding more.

Among the families that have been visiting my back yard in recent weeks, the Chipping Sparrows have the best behaved brood. They seem to have picked up the idea of feeding themselves, chipping politely on the ground as they pick up seeds which have been shoveled from the post feeder above. The Song Sparrows are next in manners, though they can often be rude toward any other bird daring to scratch on their piece of grass.

By the time the Rose-breasted Grosbeaks returned to show off their families, the young were close to being on their own. They did not do a lot of fluttering and squawking, but neither were they entirely sure what they should be doing. They moved over the feeder and investigated the suet cage, as though they knew there must be food to be had, but they weren't sure just where or how. Through random activity, they occasionally ingested food and by slow degrees they began to get the idea.

Several families of Purple Finches have come to visit. Like so many species, the young boys and girls look just like their parents; their youthfulness is betrayed by the occasional wing flutter, the feed-me posture, or a perplexed pause on the squirrel baffle when they seem to be saying, "Gee, mom and dad look like they're eating on that perch up there. I wonder where the food is coming from?"

In the trees overhanging the river, I can see fruit-and-berry loving Cedar Waxwings behaving like experienced flycatchers. They've switched diets in order to benefit from the greater protein afforded by the flying insects - important to the growth and development of the fledgling waxwing that I see being fed in the willow tree.

Of all the families of young birds which visit the back yard, the loudest, most raucous, and most entertaining, are the Blue Jays. Size alone makes them conspicuous. Add to that the blue and white display as they fly and the piercing screams that accompany their flight, and these are birds whose nearby presence cannot be missed. Watching the antics of adolescent Blue Jays makes me very sympathetic toward their parents. "Don't worry," I say to whichever of the identical looking birds are the adults, "the kids will graduate and be on their own soon. Then you'll get a little rest."

For all of the entertainment which these young bird families provide during mid-summer, there is another side. Walking toward the post feeder in the lawn, I approached to within a few feet of a Mourning Dove resting on the ground. Finally it took flight. Its passive lingering and slow response clearly showed it to be a young bird. Had I been a neighborhood cat, that dove would have learned a fatal lesson.

I find feathers strewn about the grass throughout the year, but they are more common during the summer. Sharp-shinned and Copper's Hawks are also feeder birds. In the summer these "bird hawks" also have young to feed. A young jay or dove is easy pickings, and a sumptuous meal, although these hawks are very adept at taking the experienced, but perhaps distracted and harried, adults as well.

Soon the slow moving and unwary young songbirds will serve yet another purpose. There will be adolescent hawks about, young predators who are learning to hunt. Foraging for seeds, seeking out insects, picking berries from a bush or vine is a relatively simple skill for a young songbird to learn. But the young hawk must attain a much higher skill if it is to survive. It must learn how to find, surprise, pursue and capture its food. Young birds, like the unwary Mourning Dove which I came so close to, give the young hawks a beginner's chance - like learning to hit a baseball with an underhand lob, or to putt at a two foot distance, or to cook by boiling water.

Once in a while, there will be a burst of flight from the birds around our feeders - a panic and a flash. A hawk has attacked. One late summer day, I watched a Sharp-shinned hawk streak across the backyard, twist and turn through a lilac bush in pursuit of chickadees. On that occasion, the small birds escaped and the hawk - a hatch year female - flew off to try again.

Only once have we witnessed a successful strike by a hawk. But this morning as I walked down near the river, downy gray and white feathers were stirred by my feet. To the side was a long blue and black wing feather, the remaining evidence that a Blue Jay, perhaps a young one, had been inattentive or unaware of danger - fatally so. But if it did not survive, another creature - a Sharp-shinned Hawk possibly - has extended its survival.

I may smile and laugh and find pleasing entertainment as I watch the antics of the young birds making life so frantic for their parents. But my amusement is only incidental. There are serious life rhythms at work, and we would do well to take those rhythms seriously, to protect them and preserve them. They do not exist for our dilettante-ish enjoyment, nor our exploitation, but ultimately for the welfare and preservation of this world we call home.

Ravensnest, Dummerston

CHAPTER 3

RAVENSNEST

In mid-March, I made my first visit to Ravensnest. Dense snow pack, two feet in depth, covered the ground. My snowshoes made a bare dent as I set out. The logs and roots and stumps were hidden beneath the white cover, but the large boulders on the rugged slope bulged everywhere. A rugged climb brought me to where I could see the sheer rock face across the quarry bowl. Beneath an overhang clung a huge mass of tangled sticks and branches - Ravensnest.

My vantage point was still low and I could not see into the nest. It was a sunny day which softened the deep snow and made it slick and treacherous. Caution took hold, and I did not try to climb higher for a better view. I had often seen ravens circling along the river, so I was sure that the nest was active, but no ravens were seen. I retreated down slope. As I tossed my snowshoes into the bed of the truck, from somewhere high overhead I heard the "cur-ruk" of the raven.

I returned to Ravensnest twice during the fourth week of March. The snow had been reduced to scattered patches, but those patches still made for treacherous footing and unknown traps. I circled far from the cliff edge, looking for the least steep pathway up the mountain side. Eventually I found my way to a cliff-side opening at almost the same elevation as the nest, and unobstructed by trees.

This time I could see into the nest. The female was settled deep in the nest, my view of her half obstructed by the jumble of sticks circling the rim. I was at least a hundred yards away, but clearly she knew I was there, and she was nervous about my presence. I decided not to linger.

When I reached the flats at the bottom of the mountain, I heard "cur-ruk ... cur-ruk" high overhead. I looked, and saw him circle briefly, then fly to the nest. He had waited for me to leave before drawing attention to the nest, but not without offering his opinion of my intrusion.

Ravensnest has been used by this pair for many years. Each year this bonded couple add to, and remodel, their cliff-clinging aerie during the winter months. Then sometime in early March, she lays her eggs and begins her three week incubation while he brings food to her.

On my next visit on the last day in March I had almost exactly the same experience. The female was alone on the nest, though this time she did do some moving about - which led me to think that either incubation was ending and the eggs were hatching, or that she was brooding her hatchlings. As before, her mate was unseen until I left. Then came his "cur-ruk." I was beginning to hear rude and dismissive overtones in his voice. They were probably there all along, and I was just too raven dumb to understand.

On my April 15 visit, the three chicks were big, and active. As I arrived at my viewing spot, one of the parents flew from the nest and disappeared over distant tree tops. The behavior of the chicks suggested that they had just been fed. They were noisy - still hyped up with all those new calories. But then full tummies took charge and they settled down for raven nap time. Knowing how unwelcome my presence had been in the past, I kept my visit short, though once again, back at my truck I heard "cur-ruk" from somewhere overhead.

I had a similar experience ten days later. The chicks were napping. Like any group of resting youngsters, there is always one that can't settle down. He, or she, stretched restlessly, but then gave the self up to somnolence. A parent flew quietly overhead, but otherwise both were out of sight. I did not linger. As I climbed in my truck, there was a distant "cur-ruk." I left.

Finally on the last day of April my timing was right. Three chicks, the size of their parents, were up and active. The parents' usual wariness about my presence was overcome by the need to feed their growing and demanding offspring. For their part, the chicks stretched their wings, and when a parent approached with food, their tone became loud, raucous, and chaotic. There was a "cur-ruk" or two as the parent flew off, sort of a reminder that they knew I was there and still did not like it.

A week later I visited Ravensnest again. The parents were off foraging. The kids were active and noisy. They were testing their wings, stretching and hopping. One even ventured from the nest by hopping from the stick pile to a narrow rock ledge, then back again to brag to his siblings about his daring adventure. It was obvious that they would soon fledge.

"Cur-ruk." It was the last time I heard those parting thoughts. A friend who lives a few miles from Ravensnest reported that the raven family visited his compost to glean the fresh additions on May 13. By the second week in May, the ravens had completed their nesting for the year, though they would continue to roam and forage as a family for some time.

Audubon knew ravens throughout the east in the early 1800s, but by 1900 they had virtually disappeared. In the late twentieth century they began to make a comeback and are re-occupying their former range. Interestingly, in the East they seem to be resuming their historic breeding patterns. Audubon reported that the raven's breeding season "varies according to latitude, from the beginning of January to that of June. I have found young Ravens on the banks of the Lehigh and Susquehanna rivers on the 1st of May; about tens days later on those of the majestic Hudson; in the beginning of June on the island of Grand Manan off the Bay of Fundy; and at Labrador, as late as the middle of July." The young ravens from Ravensnest visited the compost not far from the West River about the same time in May that Audubon had seen young ravens along "the majestic Hudson."

The Common Raven, also known as the Northern Raven, is the largest songbird, the largest Corvid (jays, crows, and magpies), and the most widely distributed Corvid. It is found throughout the continents of the northern hemisphere. Intelligent, wary, adaptable, resourceful, the raven has become the stuff of legend and folklore,

For now, however, I turn to the practical question asked by many: how can you tell a raven from a crow. The raven is decidedly larger, with a four foot wing span versus three foot for the crow. But we seldom see them together to compare size. Bent's *Life History* is helpful: The raven's "voice is quite distinctive ... And its flight is very different from that of the crow, swifter and less steady, with frequent turnings from side to side, accompanied by two or three rapid wing beats with occasional attempts at tumbling; its sailing or soaring flight is majestic and often used ... The four field marks by which one can most easily distinguish the raven from the crow ... are the heavy, triangular head ... the sharp break of the wings at the shoulders, the openings between the primaries, and the large fan-shaped tail."

And while that may sound simple, it does take observation and practice. When my sometime birding companion asks me, "How do you know that's a raven up there, and not a crow?" I respond with something like - "The voice, croaks not caws" ... "The way it flies" ... "The beat of the wings" ... "I just know" ... I think.

Mixed blackbird flock, mid-March, South Newfane

CHAPTER 4

SIGNS OF SPRING

The first week of March in Vermont produces three dependable signs that Spring is approaching.

The first sign is the curling plumes of smoke which rise from sugar shacks. The buckets and barrels of rising sap from the sugar maples are being converted to Vermont gold. The final product constitutes one of the basic food groups of life.

The second sign of Spring is the emergence of neighbors from their wintering dens as they congregate for town meeting, looking pale from the long weeks indoors. Some seem a bit testy, as though they were reluctantly shaking off a deep sleep. As they engage in our day of Yankee-style democracy, they are occasionally quirky, but there's nothing crazy about the way they address issues head-on.

I don't know much about the sugaring process, and further comment on town meeting probably belongs on the op-ed page. So I shall focus on the third dependable sign of approaching Spring. No, the third sign is not mud season. I've experienced enough Vermont transitions from winter to spring to know that mud season can preview in January, but rarely gets serious until late March or early April.

The third sign is, of course, the presence and activity of the birds.

During the first third of March, without fail, the black birds return: Red-winged Blackbirds, Common Grackles, and Brown-headed Cowbirds. Last Friday a huge mixed flock of blackbirds descended on my feeders, chowing down the seeds which the jays had been scattering on the ground all winter. These are common birds. They are not birds which get very many bird watchers excited, except in early March, because then they are signs of the approach of Spring.

It's not that bird watchers don't enjoy the birds that have been coming all winter to our feeders: the Black-capped Chickadee, Tufted Titmouse, White-breasted Nuthatch, Blue Jay, Mourning Dove, one sparrow or another, an assortment of finches. And it's not that we are getting tired of these familiar friends. It is that we are beginning to become restless about seeing other birds, welcoming the bursts of color and song which come with the return of the migrants. We are looking for signs that the cycles of life are intact, and in order, and functioning.

And so, in early March the bird sighting reports which appear in my e-mail from local birders and from birders around the state on the VtBird list serve, regularly report red-wings, grackles, and cowbirds. These birds have been absent, and their return is a sign of things to come.

Among the Red-winged Blackbirds, it is the male that returns first. The drab, nondescript female will come along later. For now the males are heading toward breeding territory, and soon will be claiming their piece of a swamp, or river's edge, or pond vicinity. Although very common, and sometimes even regarded as a pest, I enjoy the Red-winged Blackbird. I enjoy the enthusiasm with which the male sings from the top of a reed, flashing his red epaulets as he marks his territory and tries to attract a harem. And I appreciate the boldness with which he defends his turf, and how he joins with others to drive off potential predators.

The case of the cowbird is quite different. Ambivalence is present in the early spring reports of the cowbird: "Spring is coming. I saw my first cowbird today. Ugh." The cowbird is a brood parasite, laying an egg in one songbird nest after another and leaving the usually smaller bird to raise the cowbird young at the expense of the songbird's own young. Among most birders, to say that they dislike the cowbird is to understate the case. Distaste edging into hatred is the more likely emotion. I have seen bird watchers who are gentle pacifists toward all manner of people and circumstances, until they encounter the cowbird. Then their pupils contract to pinpoints, their lips become thin taut lines, and they whisper out curses laden with venom and the craving to administer the fatal dose.

Still ... the cowbird is a sign of spring.

"What about robins?" someone will ask. Robins are not as sure a sign of Spring as the blackbirds. I say this in spite of having heard at least three recent radio reports that Spring is approaching because a robin has been sighted. There are always some robins present throughout the winter, although they may be deep in the woods feeding on berries. These are probably the robins which breed as far north as the Arctic circle, so they are the hardy representatives of their species. The flocks of robins which wintered further south will be coming along soon, hurrying over the just-thawed ground in search of emerging protein.

Waterfowl are not as visible to most of us as are the blackbirds, but they are just about as dependable a sign of spring as the blackbirds.

Especially in the waters above and below the Vernon dam, ducks are appearing in numbers and variety. Early March is an especially fruitful time to see a variety of ducks without having to travel far. On Saturday there were huge numbers of geese, many Mallards and Black Ducks, Common and Hooded Mergansers, a few Ringed-neck Ducks, a pair of Wood Ducks, and a single Horned Grebe. The waterfowl come and go quickly, so the cast is constantly changing. They are decked in their plumage finery, and between feeding, are busy with their courtship displays.

For most of the last couple of months, birding has been dictated by watching whatever has happened to come to the bird feeders, and while birding is always good, it has not been full of variety. That is about to change, and all we have to do is stir from our winter somnolence and head outside. Even though this morning was dank and foggy, when I went out for the newspaper, the birds were singing: Tufted Titmouse "peer, peer, peer" - Northern Cardinal sweet whistle notes - nuthatch "ank, ank" - dove cooing - woodpecker drumming. In early March, the local birds know spring is coming. They begin to sing.

Chestnut-sided Warbler

CHAPTER 5

THOSE WONDERFUL WOOD WARBLERS

At 5:30 this morning, through the open bedroom window, I listened to a loud neighborhood dispute - first one, then the other, then back to the first - over and over each neighbor stated his case, made his point. The assertions went on and on, with no compromise tendered, no resolutions forthcoming.

From the cherry tree outside the window, a Chestnut-sided Warbler proclaimed his virility and boasted his genetic virtues. Further away, from the branches of a leafing ash tree, another countered his greater virility, his superior genes. Back and forth the dispute went. And somewhere nearby I was sure that one or more females were assessing the arguments, deciding which one would be best suited to help feed her young. However the pairing might be resolved, I am sure that the females will hedge their genetic bets by mating with both.

Through the day I watched as one male chased another in defense of territory, then returned quickly to a perch, and with tail cocked upward, sang the incessant and lively song - "sweet sweet sweet seesWEETchew" - or perhaps "witew, witew, witew, WEECHEW."

In his years of roaming eastern North America, Audubon only saw the Chestnut-sided Warbler one time. But with the forests cleared, and then the clearings abandoned, the Chestnut-sided has thrived. In the thickets, the young second-growth deciduous woods, and the brushy edges, it is now one of our most common warblers.

In the last few days I have heard him singing along roadways, beneath power lines, and near neglected fields. When he pauses to grab an insect and changes his perch, then I can find him with my binoculars and watch as he quivers with song. He is white underneath, with prominent chestnut sides. His back is dark, his cheeks white. He has white wing bars and a sporty yellow-crown.

I would like to tell you that there is nothing quite so breathtaking as the Chestnut-sided Warbler. But this is warbler season, the season when one must take deliberate time-outs to breath.

I was in the mountains in mixed pine, spruce, and deciduous forest. The leaves were just beginning to emerge. From the tree tops I heard a rising buzz that dropped over the top and knew that there was a northern nesting warbler overhead. He perched on a bare branch. He had a bluish back. His beak lifted, displaying his yellow throat with an orange breastband - Northern Parula. "Oh my!!" I breathed out, almost forgetting to breath back in.

There was other movement in the tree top. I moved my binoculars a half glass to the left. A burst of brilliant flame orange flared in my field of view - "Oh my!" He sang: "tsi, tsi, tsi, tsi, tsi, ti, ti, ti, ti, seeeeee." - a Blackburnian Warbler proclaiming his virtues, his flaming orange throat needing no sunlight to flash brilliantly.

Young spruce were thick and impenetrable along an old logging road, but birds were foraging through the branches, and pausing to sing a short, musical, "weeta, weeta, weeteo." One stood on the end of a spruce branch - yellow throat and breast highlighted with a thick black necklace and black streaks down his side. He flashed white wing bars and white spots on his tail. "Oh my!!" - Magnolia Warbler.

I phished to bring him out from cover. He came to investigate. Down also came a Yellow-rumped Warbler, brilliant black and white with bright yellow sides, flashing his "butter-butt" when he flew. "Oh my!! You are handsome when you dress for the ladies. I hope they're as impressed as I am."

In a brushy thicket of aspen and birch along another old logging road, "flash dancers" hurried about, long tails spread to display bright orange against black. Perching, they make me think of a miniature oriole - American Redstart. "Oh my!"

The wood warblers which inhabit our eastern forests are the envy of birders from around the world. It is no wonder ... because they are a wonder. Most spend only a few months in the north, coming up from the tropics to benefit from the rich protein resources of our temperature summers - protein in the form of mosquitos, flies, insects, creepy crawlies and such like. They come attired in their breeding plumage, breathtaking with their crisp patterns and often splashy colors.

From the higher elevations of the mountains, I came down to a marshy area in the valley where I was greeted by "sweet, sweet, I'm so sweet." The Yellow Warbler is a common inhabitant of shrubs, hedgegrows and thicket edges. He often gets short shrift from birders searching for the harder to find species. I phished him onto a branch and he scolded me, this flittering bundle of sunlight - brilliant yellow with bright red streaks on his breast and flanks. In the bright light his throat seemed to glow with a tint of orange - "Oh my!!"

And let's not overlook the Common Yellowthroat. He is as

deserving of our time as any other tree top or thicket dwelling warbler. This black-masked little rogue with the yellow throat and olive back inhabits the damp brush. He's secretive, but when agitated, he moves with the energy of the House Wren and the curiosity of a catbird. If his antics don't bring a smile to your face as he flits about and tries to warn you away, then I suspect you've got a serious case of "taking life too seriously" and probably taking yourself too seriously as well.

It's mid-morning now, and through my study window I hear the Chestnut-sided Warbler still singing, bragging to the ladies nearby. Like so many of the songbirds, there are different mnemonics suggested by different writers to help in identifying song. The most familiar mnemonic captures the cadence of song, though not necessarily the musical quality. "Please Please Please to MEETCHOU."

Yes indeed - I am pleased to meet you, too - and all the others of your family who brighten our spring woodlands.

Wood Duck, Newfane Hill beaver pond

CHAPTER 6

ON NEWFANE HILL

About a mile north of the abandoned town center on Newfane Hill is an old stone foundation, the all-but-forgotten remains from Jonathon Parks' cabin, the first permanent dwelling of the first permanent settler in Newfane. Scattered along the nearby forest lane are other foundations and cellar holes of the succession of residents who tried to make a farm living off of the hilltop in the late eighteenth and early nineteenth centuries. Then sometime later came the sheep farmers; the land was again cleared of trees and partitioned by straight stone walls marking off pasture, hayfields and woodlots. Yet again, the hilltop was abandoned and the forest returned; pines and mixed hardwoods erased all of the farmers' laborious efforts save for the stone fences, silent witness to the attempt to make the land produce for human passers-by.

Near Mr. Parks' cabin is a grove of giant maples, once tapped for their sweetness in March. Nearby also is an old apple grove, kept in respectable order by the current human borrowers of the land. But the land has not gone untended; along the old lane and between the two groves, a recent builder has reappeared to claim an ancestral right to the land. The compulsive effort of the beaver to stem the flow of water has flooded several acres of the hilltop, creating a wild pond studded with dead snags, opening the tree top canopy and inviting new life to join with him in creation and procreation.

I stood on the thick roots which splayed from the base of the white birch, leaning against the trunk for support, studying life on the pond. Mallards burst into flight from the indistinct edge of the pond as I made my unsubtle approach. Now in place, I tried to blend into the setting and become an unthreatening part of the pond life. Winged insects quickly accepted me as a welcomed food source. I protested with an occasional ineffective arm wave which was no deterrence to the insects, but a cause of concern to the hen Wood Duck. She led her brood of ducklings toward the far side of the pond and beneath protective shrubs. Only as I forced myself to remain still while being consumed, did she sense safety and allow her young to venture into the open again.

Twenty-five years ago when Vermont's first breeding bird atlas was compiled, the Wood Duck was not recorded in the Newfane block. Since then, forests have returned or matured, creating conditions suitable for beaver, who in turn have created new habitat suitable for other wildlife to colonize or re-colonize. I pulled my field card from my back pocket; next to the Wood Duck I entered the code for "downy young of waterfowl" in the "Confirmed" column.

I continued to watch unobtrusively as she ushered her seven ducklings about the pond. Most female ducks are plain, drab creatures, an adaptation that allows them to be overlooked while they incubate and care for their young. Showiness is left to the male, and none is showier or more brilliantly colorful than the drake Wood Duck. But his mate, to

31

whom he leaves all parenting responsibilities, is a remarkably handsome creature, with her subtle blue-gray head and body and bold white eye patch, patterns which blend with the trees, branches and shrubs of a beaver pond and make her almost invisible.

Mallards were scattered about the pond in pairs and threes, but none were tending to ducklings, and if any were incubating, they were camouflaged and hidden. A Magnolia Warbler sang from the thick pines behind me, and from time to time I would turn to look for it. Once they have begun nesting, they are shy, secretive and unseen. I was half aware of Red-breasted Nuthatches singing nearby, then paid closer attention when one moved on a barren snag. I became more alert when a second nuthatch made a head-first descent along the dead trunk. I was completely absorbed when one of the birds disappeared into a neat, round, and fresh nest hole. I was rapt as the pair took turns entering the hole carrying food. Again, I pulled out my field card and in the "Confirmed" column entered the codes for "adults leaving or entering nest site in circumstances indicating occupied nest" and "adult carrying food for young."

A week later I returned to the Newfane Hill beaver pond, this time stumbling my way around the pond for a different angle of view, again finding a root to stand on and a trunk to lean against. Mother Wood Duck still had her seven ducklings, significantly grown in size. Seven other Wood Duck ducklings were scattered about the pond, but if there was a mother around, I could not find her. I stayed still, blending as best I could into the scenery of the pond so that the birds could go about their business without concern.

A pair of Eastern Kingbirds were busy about the snags. On another day, I may have ticked them on a day list, or perhaps have commented privately about courtship or territorial defense. But on this day, quiet by the side of the pond, I patiently watched the female carry nesting material to the hollow top of a snag, fussily arrange her materials, try the nest out for size, and then hurry off for more material. At first it seemed her mate was merely giving directions or had other things on his mind, but she quickly put him straight and soon he was carrying materials to the nest as well.

Back on the forest lane and near the overgrown foundation of Jonathon Parks' cabin, an Eastern Wood-Pewee was perched at the end of a broken branch and singing. I sat on the grassy forest floor and watched, hoping that he would lead me to a nest, but at most he made a quick foray for food and returned to his perch. Beyond the wood-pewee a brilliant male Scarlet Tanager devotedly followed his yellow and olive-drab female as she searched the end of branches for a suitable nest site.

These species may have had a place on the Newfane hilltop 240 years ago when Jonathon Parks began clearing the forest. They had no place 120 years ago when the land was cleared for sheep pasture and hayfields. But now the forests have returned and woodland birds, so pressed in their life cycles in so many ways, at least have a place here to provide for a new generation. By slowing down and staying still, I was able to observe their efforts. In observation, I also found hope for their future.

The natural world is patient, persistent, and perseverant. On this hilltop, the natural world has rendered human presence a mere hiccup. It is a lesson in humility which we can learn willingly from the hilltop microcosm, or unwillingly from the planetary macrocosm. I prefer the willing lesson.

Ring-billed Gulls

CHAPTER 7

TRASH AND BIRDWATCHING

Once every two or three months, I throw a half dozen bags of trash in the back of my pickup and take them to the "dump," my term for the waste management center in Brattleboro. I toss them as quickly as possible into the container, and leave. The aesthetics of the place hold no attraction. The aromas contribute nothing to any kind of therapy. Even though I recycle and compost everything I possibly can, I am still appalled by the amount of trash I have generated. I handle my guilt by putting the evidence out of sight and out of mind as quickly as possible.

I grew up in a big city where plumbing had been moved indoors long before I was born. Waste disposal was very simple. All you did was flush, and it was gone - taken care of. No muss, no fuss, no smell. Since then, I've learned a little more about reality. Living mostly in small towns, I've watched borough councils impose taxes, fees, and assessments for treatment plants, and I've seen streets dug up for years to put in sewer lines. Now I live in the country and I give occasional concern to keeping my septic tank clear and my drain field healthy. I know a flush is not the end of the matter, but day by day there is not much that reminds me otherwise.

I realize that garbage and sewage are probably not topics you want to mingle with the aroma of coffee in the early morning, so I hope you are reading this during a different part of the day.

And even if it is mid-day, you may still be wondering what garbage dumps and sewage have to do with birds. The answer is quite simple. Garbage dumps and sewage treatment plants attract certain kinds of birds, and where birds gather by the hundreds, or even thousands, they attract bird watchers. People who otherwise rarely contemplate the consequences of their throw-away habits, or what happens after they flush, will gather at places where the consequences are multiplied a million-fold. They do so because there are parts of the natural world that can make a living off of our garbage and sewage.

Refuse and waste is endemic to the natural world. Leaves drop, trees die, animals defecate, animals die. All of this organic material has to be recycled and so we have microbes, dung beetles, and maggots on one end, and a host of two and four legged scavengers on the other end - a whole natural industry whose job it is to clean up the mess.

We humans have become almost supernaturally adept at creating a mess. The rest of the natural world tries to deal with our mess the best it can, but we often take exception to its efforts. For example, in the treeless barrens of a big city's downtown, there are two ubiquitous species of wildlife - pigeons in the daytime and rats at night. They can only survive because of the abundance of human-generated garbage that is available for scavenging.

Pigeons and rats don't attract bird watchers. It is also impossible for them to keep up with the megatons of garbage which are generated daily.

So at great expense, that surplus garbage and trash is hauled to landfills. Landfills attract pigeons and rats, plus other feathered scavengers like gulls and crows. Birds attract birdwatchers.

A few years ago, I did a birding trip to southern Texas, principally along the Rio Grande. One early morning, we began at the Sabal Palm Sanctuary where an old river fragment was lined with rich green vegetation and shaded by tall trees. From a bird blind we were practically on top of several dozen American Coots, a dozen Pied-billed Grebes, and several Least Grebes. The sanctuary was an Eden-like setting, a protected island that allowed us to glimpse what the land was once like.

The next stop on the birding trail itinerary (the guide book gave us precise driving directions) was the Brownsville landfill. The landfill spreads across acres and acres as it receives the throw-away refuse from a small corner of Texas. At the weigh-station, birders are asked to register and are given a map to the bird watching area, an area safely removed from the route which the trash haulers use.

There is a regular stream of birders who make the pilgrimage to the Brownsville landfill. And why? Because the garbage draws many scavenger birds, some of them unusual; occasionally a rare bird is present. Hundreds (perhaps thousands) of gulls gather at the landfill. Most are the common ones, like Herring, Ring-billed, or Laughing Gulls, but occasionally a rarity appears, like the Lesser Black-backed Gull, or the arctic-nesting Glaucous Gull. Along with the gulls are the blackbirds, like the Great-tailed Grackle and the Chihuahuan Raven. But the real attraction at the Brownsville landfill is the Tamaulipas Crow. A Mexican species, this crow wanders north of the border only on rare occasions - except at the Brownsville landfill where it regularly dines on the putrid refuse of south Texan civilization.

A North American birdwatcher who wants to tick the Tamaulipas

Crow on the life list goes to the Brownsville landfill. I did. I hauled my scope over the covered trash, endured the wind blown detritus and the odor of rancid garbage, and studied the gulls and black birds. I spent more time on the top of that dump than I collectively spend over several years at the clean and relatively odorless receptacles at our local waste management facility. Eventually I found one black bird which appeared to be a smaller and slimmer crow, decided that was sufficient to tick a Tamaulipas Crow, and left.

I was very bothered by the tons of trash I saw being trucked into the landfill. The same situation was being repeated throughout the country. I also felt quite virtuous that I fertilize with compost and make more trips to the recycling bins than I do to the dump. And I ignore the fact that, like most birders, I occasionally go to wasteful people's landfills and sewage treatment plants in the hopes of finding a bird that has not read its range map correctly.

Sometimes I wonder if my birding would be as good if all those profligate city people recycled and composted as diligently as I do. The landfills might shrink, and then where would all the birds go? Then in my more honest moments, I remember how much I haul to the dump in a year. I guess I don't really have to worry about the landfills disappearing.

(As a parenthetical by-the-way, some old-time birders in my area still miss watching the gulls at the old Brattleboro landfill.)

I still have to flush, but it goes into the septic system and remains out of sight and nose. Those city dwellers, on the other hand, not only flush, but dump everything in the kitchen sink disposal, leaving masses of sewage to be treated. Like the landfills, the treatment facilities attract birds, so sometime soon I'll take you on a birding trip to the sewage plant. I'll bet you can't wait.

House Wren

CHAPTER 8

BACKYARD PEYTON PLACE

In the mid-1950s, "Peyton Place" by Grace Metalious became a run-away best seller. It spawned a movie and a prime time television soap. By today's standards of "Desperate Housewives" and "Sex in the City," "Peyton Place" is tame. Fifty years ago it was shocking as it told a story of a small New England town rife with adultery, lust and murder. Everybody read the book, some secretly by flashlight under the covers at night - others with embarrassment that their literary interests had sunk so low.

To the embarrassment of our neighbors across the river in New Hampshire, it was soon learned that the town chronicled in the novel was a composite of three small New Hampshire towns, and that the characters were only semi-fictional.

For the boomer generation and its parents, "Peyton Place" became synonymous with scandal, with rampant lust and adultery behind a veneer of respectability - something like what goes on in our backyard all the time.

The older generations, with creative euphemisms, often explained the "facts of life" with the "birds and the bees," and especially pointed to the devotion, solicitous care, and loving fidelity which so many feathered species exhibited. With little subtlety, they conveyed the message that we, the higher species, should learn the lesson from those faithful birds, and comport ourselves with standards at least as high and at least as virtuous as those birds.

It turns out, however, that the standards and the virtues of the birds is about on the level of Peyton Place. Consider the three Mississippi Kites in a small New Hampshire town: two females and one very "busy" male. Whether you describe their situation as a menage a trois, or simply as polygamy, it is clearly not the standard which moralists would hold up as an example to follow.

But, my Vermont neighbors, let us go easy on our New Hampshire neighbors. Nor let us think that those southerners from Mississippi are infiltrating our dour New England Puritanism with the decadence of the old plantations.

Consider this 1920s report from Massachusetts ornithologist, Edward Forbush, on House Wrens which had been tagged with numbered leg bands: "one male mated with a certain female and while she was sitting on her eggs he left her and mated with another female, joining her in nesting in another box. The first female hatched her brood, fed them for a while, and then apparently became enamored of another male, brought the first male back to attend to her brood, and went away with her new lover and started another family while her first mate fed and reared her first brood. Such actions would constitute a scandal in polite society. I have heard of several instances where a male House Wren was mated with two females, each with a brood, and domiciled in

39

nesting-boxes near each other. In these cases the male divided his attentions between the two, sang mostly where both could hear him, and 'all was merry as a marriage bell.'"

Forbush seems a bit embarrassed at reporting the wren behavior, especially since so many other birds practiced the faithful monogamy he and his society expected. Unfortunately the assumed monogamy turns out to be almost non-existent.

In the early 1990s it was discovered that "many apparently monogamous birds regularly engage in extra-pair copulations, in effect 'cheating' on their mates. It was discovered, in short, that raising young together does not imply sexual fidelity." (Sibley, *Bird Life*)

As far as the birds are concerned, ornithologists have had to refine their understanding of avian monogamy to include two include distinct definitions. Pair-bonded birds can be "socially monogamous" - that is, they cooperate in raising young. They can be "genetically monogamous"; the male and female are the sole parents of all of the young they raise. Or they can be both. Or neither. The ninety percent of bird species which appear to be monogamous are socially monogamous. "Genetic monogamy may be the exception rather than the rule among birds." In other words, birds cheat on their partner routinely.

Just as DNA is used to establish paternity in humans, it is also used to establish paternity and maternity among the birds. As additional species are studied, the prevalence of extra-pair copulations continues to grow. It is not uncommon for a male songbird - solicitous, attentive, and devoted to his family - to be helping raise at least one young fathered by another male - and sometimes to be raising only one young which he fathered. While less common, a female will sometimes dump her egg in another bird's nest, leaving all parenting responsibilities for that offspring to another female of her species, and possibly another male as well.

The position of the moralists who may look to the birds for instructive lessons gets even worse. The females who step out on their mates do so willingly; they seek out other males. "Mating with additional males may allow a female to overcome the fact that her choice of mates was limited during pair formation and to produce some young fathered by a higher-quality male than her social mate." (Sibley) Or it may simply be that she is instinctively looking for genetic diversity for her brood, just as he is looking to scatter his genes as widely as possible.

Oh dear - after tittering about Peyton Place in our backyards, I have gotten scientifically serious. Well, I am a sometime citizen scientist, but mostly I am a bird watcher. And I must admit that much of the entertainment value of bird watching comes from their scandalous behavior. I get just enough glimpses of the two House Wren pairs in my backyard to know that there are things going on that would shock Peyton Place.

My goodness! - I hope the moral police and self-appointed guardians of my virtue don't get wind of what's going on in my backyard. Imagine if they turn their attention from the mind-numbing, mind-dumbing stuff that television tries to pass off as entertainment, to the wild and raucous and torrid triangles, quadrangles, and poly-tangles that keep me raptly engaged through the sensuous days of summer. Imagine if the dour moralists discovered that my good birding means watching "bad birds." They might try to bore me to virtue by making me watch some desperate housewife program instead of birds.

After grabbing a seed, a Tufted Titmouse perched in a lilac and whistled a clear, loud, "pe-ter, pe-ter, pe-ter." I know what he wants!

Shocking! ... and entertaining!

Black-capped Chickadee

CHAPTER 9

MY FAVORITE BIRDS

There was an exercise which ran through the birding blogs. It asked birders to list their ten favorite birds. I tried to make such a list, but quickly realized that it was an impossible exercise. I started with some obvious birds - like the Wood Duck or Harlequin Duck, the Rose-breasted Grosbeak or the Blackburnian Warbler. But then I had to admit that I could choose ten species from among the waterfowl alone. The Rose-breasted's family includes the cardinal, Pyrrhuloxia, Blue Grosbeak and Indigo Bunting, all of which merit a place on the list of my ten favorite birds. Among the warblers there are at least twenty species that belong among that list of ten.

The birds already mentioned jump out because of the beauty of their plumage, but that means having to skip over other criteria which are just as compelling for a favorite bird - such as the loquacity of the wrens, the acrobatic agility of the nuthatches, the aeronautic ability of the hummingbirds, the patience of the stalking heron, or the intelligence of the raven.

So I wondered if there might be a way to refine this list making. Could I make a list limited to the ten birds whose songs were my favorite songs? I began by listing the thrushes: Wood and Hermit Thrush, Veery, and for all of its familiarity, the robin. Then I added the mimics: mockingbird, Brown Thrasher, and Gray Catbird. The ethereal Common Loon needs to be on the list. There were four or five wrens that had to make the cut. The Baltimore Oriole, Indigo Bunting, and American Goldfinch deserve consideration. I love the Eastern Towhee's "drink your teeee" and the White-throated Sparrow's haunting "pooooor sam peabody peabody peabody."

Even limiting the list to favorite songsters was getting impossible. How about intelligence? Could I make a list of my ten favorite and most intelligent birds? That was almost too easy. The Corvids are, hands down, the most intelligent birds: jays, magpies, crows, and ravens. There are nineteen species of Corvids in Kaufman's guide, but only four in New England: Blue Jay, American Crow, Common Raven, and in the boreal forests an occasional Gray Jay. Remarkable intelligence among birds, just as with other higher species, is remarkable for its rarity. Listing favorite species based upon their intelligence almost seems a no-brainer.

A more manageable exercise might be the listing of my ten favorite feeder birds - those who enjoy the copious amounts of free food that I put out for them. This pares the list of choices down to about thirty-five species, and some of those can be quickly eliminated: pigeon, House Sparrow, cowbird, and starling. The list will start off with the most colorful species (or more precisely, the most colorful males): Rose-breasted Grosbeak, Evening Grosbeak, and Northern Cardinal. I would like to include the Baltimore Oriole on this list, but I have never

43

succeeded in enticing one to any feeder, although I have put out oranges until they turned black with mold. The Ruby-throated Hummingbird makes the list, as does the Blue Jay, Black-capped Chickadee, Tufted Titmouse, and the Red-breasted and White-breasted Nuthatches. The Downy and Hairy Woodpeckers with their acrobatics on the suet feeder and their faithful presentation of their young every year for my inspection are a part of this list. And how can I discriminate among the sparrows which visit or stay during the year: White-throated, White-crowned, Fox, Chipping, and Song.

Do you see the problem? I've got sixteen feeder birds on my list of ten, and I haven't even included the goldfinch whose flocks take flight from the August lawn as though the sun were exploding.

I feel badly that I haven't yet found a place for the Mourning Dove on the list of favorite feeder birds. Any creature that could fly south to warmer climes but elects to stay through our Vermont winters is worthy of inclusion.

Nor have I yet mentioned the Sharp-shinned Hawk whose hunting forays through the feeder birds provide drama, excitement, and a glimpse of the life and death struggles from which our modern lifestyles are so insulated.

Perhaps a manageable exercise might be to list my favorite families of birds. Classification of birds is a fluid, every changing science, but at present there are about seventy-seven bird families represented in North America. I haven't finalized my list, but here are some early entrants, and I am limiting myself at this time to the Passeriformes, or perching birds. On the following list, I indicate the number of North American species in the family, and a few representatives of the family which put the family on my list of favorites.

Corvidae: jays, magpies, crows, ravens - 18 species, including Blue Jay and Common Raven

Paridae: tits - 11 species, including Black-capped Chickadee and Tufted Titmouse

Trogolodytidae: wrens - 9 species, including House Wren, Winter Wren, Carolina Wren

Parulidae: wood warblers - 51 species, with too many prime representatives to list

Cardinalidae: cardinal & grosbeaks - 10 species, including Northern Cardinal, Rose-breasted Grosbeak, Indigo Bunting

Iceteridae: blackbirds - 23 species, including Baltimore Oriole, Bobolink, Eastern Meadowlark, and many other candidates, but unfortunately also including the Brown-headed Cowbird.

Tyrannidae: tyrant flycatchers - 35 species, including Eastern Phoebe and Eastern Kingbird

Mimidae: mockingbirds and thrashers - 10 species, including Northern Mockingbird, Brown Thrasher and Gray Catbird.

In choosing my favorite families of birds, I have not yet weighed the loons, waterfowl, waders, terns, or shorebirds, so I still have a lot of work to do.

In the foregoing paragraphs, I've mentioned at least forty-five species, some more than once. Some readers have probably groaned at some of the species I've included, while other readers are undoubtedly irate that I have overlooked some species.

And maybe I shouldn't bother with this exercise anymore. I think I have figured out what my ten favorite birds are ... they are the last ten birds which passed through my field of view. The dilemma is resolved!

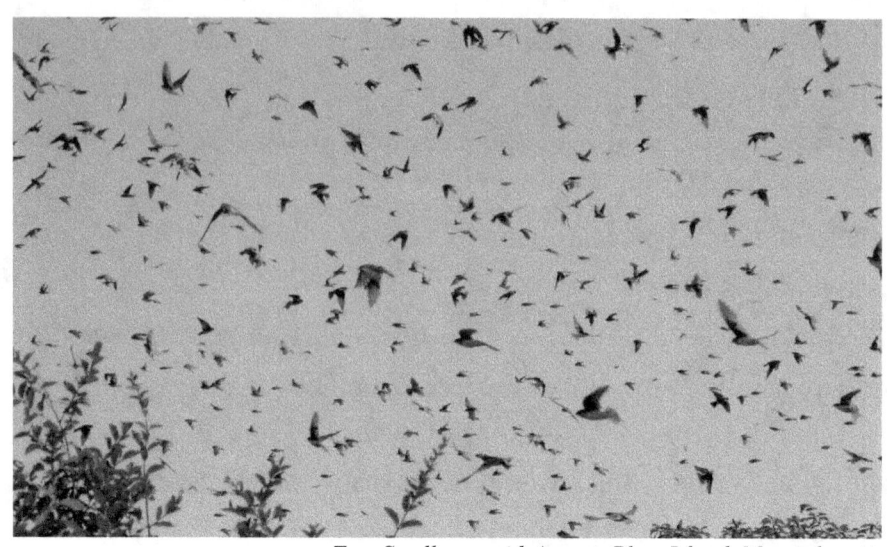

Tree Swallows, mid-August, Plum Island, Massachusetts

CHAPTER 10

WHEN BIRDS DARKENED THE SKY

At a local Audubon board meeting in August a few years ago, I announced to the group that I was going to Plum Island the next day. A couple of rare shorebirds were being reported, and I hoped to see them. The biologist-naturalist in the group declined the invitation. Ruefully he said that when he went to the shore, he liked to see birds in primordial numbers. I did not see the rare shorebirds, nor were the common shorebirds present in very great numbers. But standing between the dune and the tidal marshes, I found myself surrounded by masses of swallows. It was the peak of their Fall migration, and wave after wave, in the hundreds and thousands, swooped over the dunes, swirled through the marsh grasses, and disappeared in the distant mists as they hurried on their long journey.

At the time, I felt that I had experienced primordial numbers. The wildlife managers at the refuge estimated the numbers at ten thousand per day, for several days. But now, I am not so sure. I am not so sure that I saw primordial numbers on that day, nor that any of us can ever experience, on any day, primordial numbers. The untamed, untrammeled wilderness, an essential ingredient to wildlife in primordial numbers, is gone. Even the small pockets of reserved wilderness cannot preserve what once was, for the "taming" and "exploitation" can never be fenced out. The larger ecosystem, to use the favored term, with all of its alterations, inevitably alters the few pockets of remaining wilderness which survive from the primordial landscape.

I got a literary glimpse of what North America was like in its primeval condition when I read the biography, *John James Audubon: The Making of an American* by Richard Rhodes (Alfred A. Knopf, 2004). As a young man, Audubon emigrated from France to avoid Napoleon's draft. Looking for ways to restore the family's prosperity and make a living, Audubon subordinated his natural inclination for ornithology and art, to make his way as a merchant and importer on the western frontier. As a young entrepreneur in his twenties, he traveled the Ohio and Mississippi Rivers, eventually settling in Henderson Kentucky, opening a store, and attempting to establish a steam-driven mill. The businesses failed, and young Audubon was compelled to turn to his art to make a living - giving lessons and doing portraits. This in turn necessitated travel, and as he traveled he studied nature, painted birds, and evolved his dream of one day publishing "The Birds of America."

The first half of this biography of Audubon is also an account of the American frontier, when that frontier ended at the Mississippi River, when elk and bison could routinely be seen grazing along the banks of the mighty rivers, when wandering wolves provoked no astonishment, and when immense flocks of birds darkened the skies.

About 1813, Audubon watched Passenger Pigeons flying in a column a mile wide for three consecutive days. He estimated the

47

numbers at 1.1 billion birds, a conservative number compared to the estimate of his contemporary, Alexander Wilson, who put the number at 2 billion - still conservative by the estimate of a modern expert who numbers the Passenger Pigeon in the early nineteenth century at 3 billion, representing 25 to 40 percent of all breeding birds in America. Audubon's passing flock fed the local population for over a week, and left in its wake many wagonloads of dung.

The Passenger Pigeon existed in staggering primordial numbers - inexhaustible numbers, in Audubon's estimate. So immense was one arriving flock, that as they settled on their perches, the branches gave way under their weight, destroying hundreds of birds on and below the branch. In the course of his lifetime, Audubon saw the disappearance of the eastern wilderness, the disappearance of once abundant quadrapeds, like the elf and the bison, and game fowl, like the Wild Turkey. But he could not imagine that a mere one hundred years later, the last Passenger Pigeon would die and the species would be extinct.

Such looks into a primeval America run through Audubon's life. He encounters an immense flock of cranes, and misidentifies the gray ones as the immature offspring of the white ones. In fact, the gray cranes were Sandhill Cranes, while the white ones were the now seriously endangered Whooping Crane. From a large flock of Trumpeter Swans (endangered today, but recovering) he takes dinner and a specimen. Carolina Parakeets (extinct) are frequently encountered by Audubon and collected. Eskimo Curlew (extinct) is unremarkable among the shorebirds of Long Island. Interestingly, in all of his extensive travels, only once does he encounter a Chestnut-sided Warbler.

The most jarring aspect Audubon's life for this modern reader to accept is the way in which he studied his birds - difficult because it is so contrary to how we study them today. He shot them. That is how science was done until just a few decades ago. Without binoculars, spotting scopes, or cameras (which now provide multitudes of digital images), the only way for Audubon to study a bird, and sometimes the only way for him to identify a bird, was to hold it in the hand. One could blast a shotgun at an elusive movement in the brush and come up with a specimen, an identity, and perhaps a new species. Audubon did so routinely. He loved the birds. Sometimes he anthropomorphized their behaviors, but recognized no irony in expressing affection even as he terminated their lives. As a modern reader, that is the most difficult emotional barrier to overcome when reading this superb biography of America's icon for birds, birding, and conservation. Through his life, we also get a glimpse of what "primordial numbers" of birds really are - or were - at a time when birds darkened the sky.

Western Scrub-Jay, one of several "blue" jays

CHAPTER 11

WHY I CAPITALIZE BIRD NAMES

Readers of English are sometimes annoyed when their text gets cluttered up with a lot of capital letters. Perhaps it seems too "German" for them. Or it is disrupting to the smooth flow of the eye over the written page as it bounces over the jagged capital peaks. But birders know that capitalized common names can often avoid confusion.

First some background, and an apology for the pedantry. I'll try not to succumb too often in the pages ahead.

Birds have two names. The scientific name is in Latin and consists of two parts. The genus to which the bird belongs is the first part of the name and is capitalized. The second part of the name is the species name and is in lower case. For example, the Red-tailed Hawk is *Buteo jamaicensis*. In the literature, the Latin scientific name is usually in italics, bold face, or quotations.

The scientific name is unique to each species, and because it includes the genus to which the species belongs, it also identifies relationships. For example, in North America there are two eagles, Bald Eagle, *Haliaeetus leucocephalus,* and Golden Eagle, *Aquila chrysaetos*; the scientific names tell us that they belong to two different genera. Or, consider three locally resident hawks: the Red-tailed Hawk, *Buteo lineatus,* the Sharp-shinned Hawk, *Accipiter striatus,* and the Cooper's Hawk, *Accipiter cooperi.* The Sharp-shinned Hawk and Cooper's Hawk are closely related, as the genus name indicates, while the relationship of the Red-tailed Hawk is a more distant relationship. All three are called "hawks."

The scientific name helps avoid confusion and readily tells relationships. But few of us are conversant in Latin. And some of us are tongue-challenged. I sometimes have difficulty wrapping my tongue around an unfamiliar English word. Non-English words are very likely to leave me tongue-tied. That's where the second name for birds is so helpful. In North America, the American Ornithological Union determines the genus classification and species name (the scientific Latin name), and they also determine the common name, the name by which we know our birds.

The common name does not give us information about relationships, but it does specify a particular species, with a particular scientific name. Because our language is the way it is, confusion is a serious risk. To avoid confusion, in most popular and scientific birding literature (magazines, books, monographs, reports), the common name is capitalized.

At this point, the birding world clashes with the mavens of literary usage and style. The latter prefer to see capital letters restricted to proper names and places and the beginning of sentences. When the birding world enters the broader literary world, the precision of capitalized common names disappears, and the Tufted Titmouse becomes the tufted titmouse.

David Sibley capitalizes the common names of birds when he writes his books and the articles which appear in many birding magazines. But when his syndicated column on birds goes to the newspapers, the capitals disappear. If it happens to a prominent writer like Sibley, then I can hardly object when it happens to me in my newspaper column.

Let's look at some of the confusion that could result from uncapitalized common names. For example, the jays in North America. There are ten species whose common name includes "jay." Most of these jays are blue, but there is only one Blue Jay. The Blue Jay is closely related to one other blue jay, the Stellar's Jay (genus *Cyancitta*). Our eastern Blue Jay is less closely related to five other species of blue jays in the genus *Aphelocoma*, most of which are western jays.

The Blue Jay is a beautiful bird; it flashes its blue and white patterns as it hurries about its business. Here is the East such a pattern can only be one bird. On rare occasions, we might hastily call a blue flash a bluebird (meaning Eastern Bluebird), but size, shape and behavior are unlikely to sustain such a mis-identification for very long.

It is a different story when we head out west, where the western limits of the Blue Jay overlap with eastern limits of the western jays. There we discover that the Blue Jay is not even the bluest of the jays. That distinction belongs to the Pinyon Jay, which is dull blue all over.

When I made my first trip to California, I was introduced me to the Pacific population of the Western Scrub-Jay. There are currently two sub-species (sometimes called "races") of the Western Scrub-Jay. The interior race has a pale, dull blue color; it is shy and inconspicuous. The Pacific population has darker, richer coloring; its blue is a deep blue. It is noisy and conspicuous on the West Coast, much like the eastern Blue Jay is in our neighborhoods. (Consideration is being given to splitting the two sub-species of the Western Scrub-Jay into separate species.)

On several occasions in California I saw the deep blue back of a blue bird as it flew into a tree and landed. Since I am conditioned to birding in the East, my mind processed such quick glimpses as bluebird. Then my lumbering mental processor eliminated Eastern Bluebird (way out of range) in favor of Western Bluebird, or less likely, Mountain Bluebird, both of which are beautiful blue, western bluebirds. When I put my binoculars on the blue bird which had flashed into the tree, on every occasion it was a Western Scrub-Jay (Pacific population), who immediately mocked me with a raucous call.

We did see Western Bluebirds on several occasions, and on one occasion watched a flock of several hundred Mountain Bluebirds moving through a vast field of grapevines. These sightings of the two western species of bluebirds were in habitats shunned by the Western Scrub-Jays.

Back in our neighborhoods, in the Spring and Summer, I expect to see several types of blue birds: Eastern Bluebird, Indigo Bunting, Black-throated Blue Warbler, and Blue Jay.

Through the early Spring migration, there are many different kinds of brown sparrows scratching on the ground and scarfing my bird seed. Not a single one of those sparrows is a Brown Sparrow, because there is no such bird with that common name. But most sparrows are brown.

Let's turn next to the black birds. By mid-May, two black birds are far into their annual breeding, both in the family *Corvidae*. The Common Raven is fledging its young, while the American Crow is feeding its young. At the same time, other black birds are about to nest: the Red-winged Blackbird along every river, stream, pond, and puddle - the Common Grackle in farmlands, groves, and streamsides - the Rusty Blackbird in a few high elevation coniferous bogs - and the Brown-headed Cowbird wherever it can find a nest to dump an egg. Then there are blackbirds in the blackbird family, *Icteridae* (Family, not Genus) that aren't black, like the Baltimore Oriole (*Icterus galbula*) and Eastern Meadowlark *(Sturnella magna)*.

The practice of capitalizing the common names of animal species (specifically, birds) is not mere affectation. It is an attempt to be consistent so that when the confusing names and descriptions do occur, clarity can prevail without resort to parenthetical Latin names. Finches visit our feeders in the winter, but are they Purple Finch, House Finch, or American Goldfinch? A European Goldfinch occasionally shows up somewhere in the East; otherwise our eastern goldfinches are all American Goldfinches. In the southwest, goldfinches may also be Lesser Goldfinch or Lawrence's Goldfinch.

You've just had a feeder visit from a nuthatch, but was it a White-breasted Nuthatch or a Red-breasted Nuthatch?

Whatever you call them, have fun as you watch the birds. Good birding!

Hermit Thrush, Vermont's state bird

CHAPTER 12

BIRDING THE TOWN OF STRATTON

I've been spending quite a bit of time in the Town of Stratton recently. I've been surveying a five kilometer square area, documenting breeding birds for the Vermont Breeding Bird Atlas project. Most of the survey work has been done along the few roads in the area. Occasionally I've wandered along old trails or waded into an old beaver pond. Most of the area is forested. Often the forest is young and the small trees present an almost impenetrable barrier. Aside from the scattering of homes along the roads (and many of those are second homes), the area has few residents. And yet, again and again I see signs of the past changes which have been made upon the landscape and the persistence with which nature reclaims itself and changes itself.

At the road's dead end, a track continued through the woods to a barrier which barred further travel by motorized vehicles. As I turned off the engine, I caught movement near a rotting stump littered with leaves and branches. A male Blackburnian Warbler was foraging through the debris, his beak filled with grubs and bugs. He flashed his brilliant orange throat, disappeared behind a log, then reappeared with yet more food. He flew off on a straight line flight to his nest with its hungry nestlings.

When the Blackburnian disappeared, I got out and stood still. Most of the forest around me was young and in such a situation birding is more a matter of listening than watching. But, where I stood, the woods were a little more open. To one side I noticed a depression in the ground with stones that suggested they had once had an order - an old cellar hole. Thirty yards beyond were more stones with an order to them. I went over to inspect. It was another foundation, much larger - perhaps the foundation of a barn. A ten inch tree grew from the middle, while all around smaller trees competed for light against the dense canopy. It wasn't so very long ago, 50 or 75 or 100 years ago perhaps, that this tiny settlement had been abandoned and the forest began its reclamation project. Somewhere in the deep woods, a Swainson's Thrush sang, availing itself of the regenerating conifers in the mixed forest.

From a stand of older hemlocks on the other side of the narrow lane, a Brown Creeper sang. I went in search of this elusive forest waif, this tiny bird that clings to and blends into the tree trunks. If one is lucky and observant, it might be seen creeping upward in search of food, like "a piece of bark come to life"(Kaufman). A few times I've seen the creeper with a family of recently fledged young, or spotted it as it disappeared into its nest beneath loose bark on an old pine. But not this day. This day it stayed hidden on the other side of the trunks as it sang its brief song. Some describe the song as meadowlark-like, but it's so brief that it seems as though it were almost embarrassed about drawing attention to itself.

At its peak in the mid-1800s, the Town of Stratton had a population of around 360. In 1960, the population was 24. Today the permanent population is about 150. Not many of those live in the area I've been surveying. The few who do occasionally try to maintain the gnarled old apple trees which once provided some of the subsistence living to the residents. A few of the old apple orchards are being kept clear (sort of) to provide food and habitat for deer and grouse, and incidentally, bird species that like, or need, more open space - hummingbirds, phoebes and a couple of warblers and sparrows. Most of the orchards are being taken over by the forest; the old apple trees are still competing for sunlight, but as the canopy spreads above them they will eventually lose the fight. The Ruby-throated Hummingbird, Chestnut-sided Warbler, and American Redstart will have to go elsewhere, while the Black-throated Green and Black-throated Blue Warblers and Swainson's Thrush will take over completely.

Vermont did its first breeding bird atlas twenty-five years ago. The atlas project currently underway has already documented landscape changes as evidenced in the birds which are breeding. There are fewer grassland species, as open land has been abandoned or has continued to grow up.

Those species which favor the thick, scrubby brush which first covers abandoned open land will certainly show changes as well. I went up a barely discernible, grassy lane, chasing the song of a Nashville Warbler, hoping also to hear the song of the uncommon Mourning Warbler. The lane opened onto an acre sized patch of blackberries or raspberries. But these were already giving way to willow bushes, and aspens were beginning to rise above the four foot berries. An abandoned house sagged forlornly in a corner of the clearing. There were still mattresses on the beds and beer cans in the sink. But few panes of glass remained in the windows and the decrepit building was clearly losing its grip. How long before the elements collapsed a section of roof giving light and space for a tree to grow?

I wonder what the bird life was like 150 years ago, when this hill town was at its peak, when the residents had cleared much of the forest and tended their orchards, relocated field stones into long stone walls and scratched their living from the thin soil. It was surely much different from today as the forest continues to reclaim and reestablish itself.

Conservation is tricky and complex. I am sort of a tree-hugger. I want to preserve the environment. But what do I want to preserve? As I surveyed in Stratton for breeding birds, I continually confronted evidence that the way the forest is now, is not the way it was 50 or 100 years ago, nor is it the way it will be some years in the future. I decry the clearing of forest for a long lane to a second home castle, but then I came upon an old stone foundation in a second growth forest; twisted apple trees still held on not far off. Humans constantly change the landscape and the flora and fauna ebb and flow with every change.

In a selectively logged mixed forest near one of Stratton's old cemeteries, recently fledged Hermit Thrushes were calling for food. The parents were hurrying in every direction to accommodate the demands of their brood. Vermont's state bird and premier vocalist breeds in mature mixed forest. It prefers forest with open understory. The logging had created the perfect habitat for the thrush. On my field card for the breeding bird atlas, by Hermit Thrush I entered the code, "FY" (for "feeding young") in the confirmed column.

Evening Grosbeak

CHAPTER 13

NOT CUTE

I am probably going to offend my favorite companion, family, many friends (both birding and non-birding), and many readers who put down good money for this book. I am going to raise my voice against the use of a tiny adjective, especially when that adjective is applied to birds and other wildlife. The offending word is "cute," as in, "Isn't that baby woodpecker cute?" - or - "Those baby geese are so cute."

First, I should put this language exercise into context, admitting right off that my aversion to "cute" is much, much less than my aversion to some other commonly used words and phrases. For example, to my ear the use of "actually" is like squeaky chalk on a blackboard (if there are such things as blackboards anymore). There are very few situations when this word is appropriate, but it is sprinkled liberally into many conversations. If it were salt on food, it would send blood pressures soaring. It is totally superfluous and meaningless.

As is "you know." On one level, it might mean "You don't know, but I will tell you." More likely it means that none of us know anything and there will be no enlightenment added to anyone during the course of this conversation.

Complex language is one of the few things which distinguish homo sapiens from the other animals. (But note the irony that we call ourselves "sapiens - wise" in the face of so much evidence to the contrary.) Yet, so often, rather than contributing to communication, our use of language obscures, prevaricates, or simply fills the air with noise.

Politicians provide me with a lot of language peeves. The previous leader had various renditions of "People gotta know ..." I always heard him silently adding, "... cause I don't have a clue."

Or the politicians who say, "Let me be perfectly clear," which usually means that the darkness is about to descend. Our current leader seems to be an exception with the clarity of what he says, but I suspect it is only a short time before reality and compromise may make him wish he were not always so clear.

"Everything is on the table" ... causing the table to collapse.

Somewhere down the list from these and other nonsense words and phrases which contribute nothing to communication or which simply do not apply, comes the word "cute."

The venerable Oxford English Dictionary tells me that "cute" is shortened from "acute," and means clever, keen-witted, sharp, and shrewd. This is quite different from contemporary American usage which means something like "attractive by reason of daintiness or picturesqueness." Overtones of simple, funny, adorable, and sweet are all present in the contemporary "cute."

When "cute" is applied to a bird, for example, it is never done with the sense of the bird being keen-witted or shrewd. In fact, the opposite is the case. Consider ...

Young birds only a few days out of the nest are common around my feeders as I write. The young Evening Grosbeaks are chasing their parents from feeder to tree to feeder to tree. I watched one youngster try to perch on the wrought iron plant hanger. It tried to beg for food, flutter its wings, and cling to its perch, all at the same time. It could not hold on to its perch and slid down the curved iron, nearly getting tangled in the loop at the end. When it followed dad to the platform feeder, it managed better. Wings fluttered, beak agape, its posture low and begging. Dad cracked open sunflower seeds and fed them into the open beak. Cute?

Yesterday I watched a very young female Hairy Woodpecker crawl over the suet feeder. She had some vague idea that food could be had, but she had not yet learned to peck through the openings and pick out the food. On the suet feeder at the same time was a young male Downy Woodpecker. He had the food mystery solved and was picking out pieces for himself. The bigger Hairy often caused the smaller Downy to retreat temporarily. The young Hairy kept looking at the Downy, as though she was expecting another bird with food to feed her. Cute?

For domestic reasons, I hesitate to tell you that the word "cute" was used, or is ever used, of such observations. Unfortunately, "cute" does get used even though it does not apply. There is nothing acute, clever, or shrewd about these young birds. These birds are not "cute," they are "clueless." If those young birds do not quickly solve the problem of feeding themselves while at the same time being alert to danger, they are not going to survive. No amount of imagined funny or adorable "cuteness" is going to change that.

If you insist on calling a bird "cute," in the sense of adorable or sweet, I would suggest that you also hope it gets over its cuteness quickly, because that kind of cuteness is not what it needs to survive.

Inherent prejudice also weighs in, even here in Vermont where the citizenry is decidedly liberal and tolerant. "Cute" will be applied to young woodpeckers, grosbeaks, nuthatches, titmice, chickadees, or cardinals - all "good" birds. But suppose a family of "bad" birds comes around - like starlings. Of the starlings you will not hear the word "cute." More likely you will hear adjectives like obnoxious, ugly, or greedy. The starling young, however, are just as clueless as all of the other "cute" young birds that come around. They are learning how to survive. But Vermonters, too, have their prejudices.

Starlings are birds we love to hate. Consider, however, that it may be more appropriate to apply "cute" to the starling than to most other birds. Starlings have been acute and clever in adapting to all manner of ecological niches. In North America, the European Starling has been amazingly successful - arguably as successful as the homo sapiens species that loves to hate it. Perhaps that's the reason for our enmity of the "cute" starling - we can't imagine anything else being as "cute" (clever) as we are. Life is full of self-delusions.

Please don't misunderstand me. There are appropriate uses of the word "cute." If you say to someone, "You are cute" - you might mean, "You are acute, sharp, clever." Or, you might also mean, "You are adorable."

Or, you might mean both ... As when I walk into a room wearing my new puffin t-shirt and my favorite companion says to me, "You are cute."

I do hope you enjoy all those not cute birds.

Harris' Hawk

CHAPTER 14

WHAT IS A RAPTOR?

I give up! I have been trying to find a more-or-less scientific definition which will apply to all of the birds commonly called raptors, and I can't do it.

There are two types of birds commonly called raptors. The nocturnal raptors are the owls; the diurnal raptors are the hawks. It is the latter group which causes the confusion. Well known writers on birds, such as David Sibley (*Guide to Birds*) or Scott Weidensaul (*Raptor Almanac*) include in this category hawks, eagles, falcons, and vultures, or more specifically, the birds which are classified in the families *Accipitridae, Cathartidae,* and *Falconidae.*

In the simplest and broadest sense, raptors are birds of prey, which means that they prey on other living creatures for their food; they are meat eaters. But nearly all birds are at least part-time birds of prey. Swallows swooping through the sky and consuming insects are birds of prey. Robins pulling worms out of the grass are birds of prey. Nuthatches and brown creepers picking insects out of bark, or chickadees and warblers finding caterpillars on the undersides of leaves, are birds of prey. Mergansers and cormorants diving for fish are birds of prey. Shrikes are skilled predators whose prey includes small vertebrae, birds, mammals and reptiles, all of which sound like the diet of a raptor, except that the shrikes are songbirds.

Moreover, not all raptors are birds of prey. The Turkey Vulture dines on carrion. It does not catch and kill its food, but waits for other forces to kill a creature which it then seeks out with its keen sense of smell. The Black Vulture occasionally kills its food, but this typically happens with an animal that is already severely injured or sick - that is, in the process of dying.

There is yet another problem with the vultures. Old World vultures are closely related to the hawks and falcons, and for a long time New World vultures were also considered to be closely related. But DNA studies have recently shown that New World vultures are really short-legged storks ... or maybe something else. They are not even second or third cousins of the hawks.

I posed the question to a raptor specialist: how would you define "raptor?" Carefully he gave this definition: "A raptor is a bird of prey which captures and kills its food in its specially adapted talons." Note that he used the indefinite article, "a," in recognition that most birds are in some sense birds of prey.

When I then asked him about the vultures, his response was: "Vultures aren't raptors. They don't have the specially adapted talons; they don't capture their food, and they aren't even related." That is certainly one way of dealing with the a sticky inconsistency.

Playing the devil's advocate, I said: "What about the eagle when it steals a fish from an Osprey? It hasn't captured food."

"No, but it uses its specially adapted talons to carry it off."

"How about the eagle that feeds on a deer carcass during the winter? It neither captures it, nor carries it away in its talons."

Reply: "It was opportunistic. That doesn't negate the definition."

Then I asked: "How about the Northern Caracara?" The caracara is a member of the falcon family that feeds mainly on carrion which it finds by flying low over the southern savanna or desert. "Or the Hook-billed Kite?" I continued. In Texas we saw trees covered with small snails, and on the ground, snail shell debris, the remains of the prey of the hook-billed kite, a prey that was not captured in its talons.

At this point the raptor specialist pointed out a Sharp-shinned Hawk in pursuit of a bird, and soon after that further diverted my attention to a soaring Red-tailed Hawk.

Watching the soaring Red-tailed Hawk, I wondered if raptors might be defined by their flying ability. The Red-tail is a master of the wind. I have often watched a Red-tail hovering over Putney Mountain, fixed in one spot in the sky, only occasionally making a slight wing adjustment to maintain its position as it hunts for prey. Or the Broad-winged Hawks - capable of traveling dozens of miles without a wing-beat as they ride the thermals and wind currents. Or the eagles and Ospreys, gliding steadily through strong, gusting winds, impervious to the buffeting that grounds other birds. Defining raptors by their flying ability would certainly allow for inclusion of the vultures with their masterful flying abilities.

But alas, that doesn't work either. As accomplished in the wind and on the wing as the raptors are, they have no edge on many pelagic birds, some of which spend their entire life in the air except when nesting. When a Black-footed Albatross takes flight for the first time, it stays aloft for the next three years. Or consider the Arctic Tern: between nesting seasons in the far north, it travels 22,000 miles, most of the time far from shore.

The best summary that I have been able to find is that raptors are defined anatomically by feet and beaks which are specially adapted for hunting, even though they may not use them for that purpose. The vultures have neither, but are included with the raptors because ... well, just because.

A long suffering spouse of a dedicated hawk watcher offered this definition: "A raptor is what the bird nerds on Putney Mountain are hoping to see during September and October." That's not very scientific, but I know exactly what that means!

Red-bellied Woodpecker

CHAPTER 15

WHATEVER YOU CALL THEM

I once had an e-mail from a reader who reported a Red-bellied Woodpecker at his bird feeder. Then he mused, "I wonder where names like this come from....shouldn't it be Red-back-part-of-head Woodpecker? Why Rose-breasted Grosbeak instead of red-breasted? Why Red-breasted Nuthatch instead of rose, or reddish tan?"

His questions could serve as an English teacher's example of a conundrum. Why the common names of birds are what they are is a mystery. To be sure, the Red-bellied Woodpecker does have a red-belly, but it is almost never seen in the field, even by those who see and study the bird frequently. The red-belly can be found when the bird is being held in the hand, and the prominent white feathers on the belly can be parted to reveal the underlying red. Hardly a dominating field mark! It has a black and white zebra-like back, prompting some people some place some time to call it the Zebra Woodpecker. Or how about one of its other folk names? - the wonderfully mysterious, "Cham-chack." "I saw a Cham-chack at my feeder today!" That conveys a life, an excitement, that sends "red-bellied" to a place on the bench reserved for fourth string players.

Continuing my e-mailer's musings: Why Rose-breasted Grosbeak instead of red-breasted? Good question. I have described the brilliant red throat which barely descends to the breast as blood-red. Roses come in all kinds of colors, but the red rose is the special domain for the lover wooing his lady-love. The "red-rose" -breasted Grosbeak is like a feathered Romeo who full throatedly serenades his Juliet in the Spring. But alas, he is spurned, and he bleeds a great drop from his broken heart. Then there is the folk name reflective of a time when violence was more common place: "Throat-cut." Imagine also a more rural time when your survival depended upon the produce of your garden; you wage a constant battle against the insect vermin. Potatoes are especially susceptible to certain bugs. You notice a bird foraging through your potato patch. You don't much care about the brilliant red throat or the bold black and white wings. You may even be seeing the dull brown female of the species. But you are glad to have the "Potato-bug Bird" helping in the fight against the potato bugs.

To my thinking, bird names lack imagination, beauty, and poetry. They also lack consistency, and often sense. But there seem to be some criteria that apply ... some of the time. For example, there is geography. The Northern Cardinal is the only cardinal to range as far north as Canada; others are tropical or sub-tropical. Our cardinal's only other North American relative is found along the southern U.S. border, the Pyrrhuloxia, a bird with a name that is unpronounceable and of mysterious origin. Or there is the Carolina Chickadee, a bird of the southern states (including especially, I suppose, the Carolinas). It has a black-cap and looks almost exactly like the Black-capped Chickadee of our area. The name of the latter is based on a characteristic of its plumage which it shares with the Carolina Chickadee. (Redundancies noted!)

The Tufted Titmouse is a close relative of the Black-capped Chickadee and also has a name based on a distinguishing feature of its plumage - its "tufted" crest. But, all four North American titmice have tufted crests. However, the Oak Titmouse of California prefers oak habitat, while the Juniper Titmouse of the southwest prefers juniper habitat. Habitat preference, you might correctly conclude, is yet another criterion that sometimes applies when naming a bird. I have no quarrel with the name, Tufted Titmouse, but I also like the folk name: Peter-bird. With the first signs of a break in winter, you can hear the cheerful song of the Peter-bird: "peter, peter, peter."

Another criterion is hemisphere: for example, American Robin, American Redstart, and European Widgeon (The last is a rare but regular North American visitor.) And then there is commonalty: Common Loon (not so common until recent conservation efforts), and Common Merganser (sometimes outnumbered by Hooded Merganser in our waters). Our local snipe use to be "common," until it was split from its European relative and resumed its former name, Wilson's Snipe. Alexander Wilson was America's first true ornithologist; the birds bearing his name (plover, warbler, storm-petrel, phalarope) may have been first identified by him, and later named in his honor. That is yet another criterion sometimes used in naming birds - if you discover it, you can name it - after yourself if you have a rampant ego, or after a friend, mentor, lover, or whoever ... or whatever.

The naming of birds is fickle and inconsistent. The Baltimore Oriole (which sports the colors of Lord Baltimore, founder of Maryland) and Bullock's Oriole (I don't know who he was) were lumped into one species as the Northern Oriole. Then they were split and we again have the Baltimore Oriole and the Bullock's Oriole. The Rufous-sided Towhee and the Western Towhee were lumped to become the Rufous-sided Towhee, then they were split to become the Eastern Towhee and the Spotted Towhee.

Presumably, when a single species is split into two or more species, the names assigned to the new species are "new" so as to prevent confusion with the old names. Hence the disappearance of the Rufous-sided Towhee. (Alas!) But when the Canada Goose was recently split into two species, confusion was allowed to reign: the new species are Canada Goose and Cackling Goose. Is there not a saying that attributes consistency to the small-minded?

The Rock Dove has finally been recognized for what it is and has been renamed the Rock Pigeon. Long before these birds became urban pests, they nested in caves in rocky precipitous cliffs. They still nest is such places, even though there may be no natural stone in sight: on bridges, in bell towers, building cornices, copulas. The "rock" in Rock Pigeon is an historical reminiscence.

So who's responsible for the bird names? Or if you prefer, who's to blame? The American Ornithological Union has the responsibility in North America. Their efforts may provide outside observers like myself with limitless material for a weekly column. But, the AOU imposes an order and consistency across the continent which allows Vermonters to converse with Texans about a bird without having to sort through different names for the same bird. There's enough problem with the way those people use their vowels and clip their syllables.

But listen. I've got an ank-ank and a topsy-turvy at my feeders, so I've got to go. Good Birding - whatever you call them.

Birders on a "chase"

CHAPTER 16

THE DIRTY SECRET OF CHASING BIRDS

In mid-January, an Ivory Gull was seen in Gloucester, Massachusetts. It was the first record of this rare arctic gull in Massachusetts. With all of the modern communication means available, the gull instantly attracted bird chasers eager to add a new tick to the life list. I was in Arizona, so I could not join the chase, but I know at least five people from the Brattleboro area who drove to the coast on a weekend to chase the bird. I have no doubt that there were chasers who flew to Boston from around the country. Many others drove several hundred miles to join the chase.

At the eastern point of the Gloucester Harbor there is a Coast Guard station and a lighthouse. At the point, there is also an Audubon bird sanctuary, and a small parking lot with enough parking space for about ten cars. Birders are often found scanning the calm waters of the harbor and the ocean waves beyond the breakwater. Stopping there on a winter

71

coastal birding trip, I always see a few other birders enduring the cold wind in hopes of picking up an unusual bird.

At that eastern point in January, the Ivory Gull was spotted. On a Saturday in January, there were five hundred people gathered at Lighthouse Point, hoping to see the Ivory Gull and add a very rare tick to their North American life list. Five hundred people means a lot of automobiles. The narrow road to the point goes through an up-scale shore community before finally reaching the bird sanctuary. You can imagine the traffic and parking problems. It was so bad that eventually someone called the police to give instructions about clearing the road.

Fortunately for the crowds of bird chasers, the Ivory Gull arrived before the police did. It put on a flight demonstration, then rested on the breakwater and gave very satisfying views to the massed bird chasers. As I have talked with people who made the successful chase, their excitement is still palpable, not to mention their gloating.

Chasing birds can be fun. I remember one summer when I went to the Connecticut shore to see a Red Stint, a small sandpiper. Three days later I went to Plum Island to see a Black-tailed Godwit. A couple of weeks later, there was another spontaneous trip to Kittery, Maine, for a Western Reef-Heron from Africa. I saw many of the same people at each location - New England birders in close touch with one another, monitoring the resident birds while keeping their eyes open for rarities and vagrants.

But, there is a dirty secret about chasing birds - a secret which the bird chasers don't want to admit to, or may not even be aware of.

An ecologist friend recently estimated the carbon footprint when he drives to the coast. He estimates that he puts about fifty pounds of carbon into the atmosphere on a round-trip to the Massachusetts coast. Global warming is caused by putting vast amounts of carbon into the atmosphere. By some estimates, global warming will soon put as many

72

as thirty percent of all vertebrate species in danger of extinction. (Birds are vertebrates; so are we.)

Now come the tough questions. Should birders, who love birds, be contributing to their potential extinction just for the ego-satisfying opportunity to add another check to their life list?

At the extreme, there are people so intent upon maintaining their place on the list of top listers, that upon hearing the report of a rare species, they immediately drive to the airport, book a flight and rental car, and set off. But when I hop in my car when a vagrant pops up on the list serve, am I that different, except in degree?

Like all moral issues in life, the answers are gray. Birders have, and are, making significant contributions to conservation efforts, and to local economies. To give one example: Cape May, New Jersey, is a seashore resort. In today's economy, a business needs to do business for more than just a few months in the summer. The Cape May Bird Observatory has been very successful in communicating the economic contribution which birders make to Cape May economy. This contribution often comes during slower months for the seaside resort - months when bird migrations make southern New Jersey a place of pilgrimage for bird watchers: April and May, September to November. If the habitat which the birds depend upon is not maintained, then the birds won't be there, and neither will the bird watchers and their credit cards. Local support for birds and habitat conservation and restoration among the business community in Cape May has grown significantly over the past few decades.

Birders also wander through and monitor the birds in their immediate neighborhoods. They report birds that are extending their range, or becoming more difficult to find. They count species and identify "Important Bird Areas" (like Herrick's Cove or Rutland Marsh), and that in turn leads to protection and conservation.

Wetlands have been preserved, grasslands restored, and forests protected, because birders have prowled their neighborhoods (I am willing to define "my neighborhood" as New England), looking for birds, noting migration dates, population trends, and habitat changes. Even while birders are contributing hydrocarbons to the atmosphere and threatening the long-term existence of many species, they are also providing information and support for conservation efforts (and economies) without which many birds would more quickly be swept to extinction.

Bird lovers and nature lovers claimed a moral high ground when they raised voices against the polluters of waterways, the dumpers of toxic wastes, and the rapers of forests. The dirty secret we don't want to acknowledge as we drive about enjoying nature, watching birds, and being proud of the waste dumps we helped to get cleaned up, is that we have met the enemy (in the words of that modern philosopher, Pogo) and he is us.

There is truth (even if it is said with a smirk) in the adage: Save water - shower with a friend. By extension, bird with a friend. You'll both see birds and you will cut your per person carbon footprint in half. Or bird with two friends, and cut your footprint by a third.

Now I wonder, how long will it be before I fall off my moral high horse?

Black Scoter on a Newfane Village pond

CHAPTER 17

BLACK SCOTER VISITS NEWFANE

About a week before Thanksgiving, a neighbor alerted me to a Black Scoter that was hanging out in the small pond across from the Four Columns Inn in the village of Newfane. I hurried up the road and enjoyed the treat of watching an adult male moving about the peaceful surface as he preened himself, a daily task of feather maintenance.

The Black Scoter is a diving duck. I have seen hundreds of them. At a sea watch site in Avalon, New Jersey, where migrating waterfowl are counted, I saw line after line of scoters flying just above the water's surface a quarter mile offshore. In half an hour, hundreds flew south along the coast.

Black Scoters are common during the wintering months off the Atlantic coast. They are often in mixed flocks with Surf Scoters and White-winged Scoters. On my two or three winter coastal birding trips, I usually need my binoculars to find them bobbing in the off-shore surf.

A decent view requires my scope with its eyepiece at full 60x zoom, and even then the views are brief. I no more than find them and focus, and the birds dive, pop back to the surface, and dive again.

But this scoter in Newfane was in the middle of a small pond, perhaps fifty feet from the pond's rim. I used my binoculars to look at him, but I did not really need them to see his stiff upright tail, his sleek black plumage, and his most distinguishing feature - the "orange 'golf ball' balanced on the base of his bill" (the description which Pete Dunne gives to the prominent bump).

Scoters feed primarily on mussels, diving to depths up to forty feet. The Black Scoter also takes small sea-clams and scallops, and on inland ponds or lakes, it takes fresh-water clams. The Black Scoter on the Newfane pond was seen diving. I have no idea about clams being in the pond, but like most species, the Black Scoter will feed on whatever is available, including aquatic plants.

Forbush describes the Black Scoter as "tough, hardy, a quick and excellent diver ... It can swim a long distance under water and uses both wings and feet at need for under-water progression."

Black Scoters are arctic breeders. The eastern population nests in Quebec and Labrador east of the Hudson Bay. Audubon found a nest six feet from the edge of a large fresh water pond about a mile from the shore of the Gulf of St. Lawrence. When breeding is complete, they head south along the Atlantic coast and major river valleys.

Lake Champlain and the Hudson River Valley is a significant flyway for scoters. In late October, I stopped at Oven Bay in Addison where lake counts are often done. Far off shore was a raft of about forty scoters. Each of the three scoters - Black, Surf, and White-winged - were identifiable in the raft, but that's about all. One could hardly say that the view of these scoters was satisfying. It was nothing like the rare, close-up opportunity, to observe the Black Scoter on the Newfane pond.

The scientific name for the Black Scoter is *Melanitta nigra*, from the Greek, *melas*, "black" and *nitta*, "duck," and the Latin, *nigra*, "black." The common name is more interesting. Scoter seems to be a variation for "coot." In Middle English, "coot" was used for various waterfowl, including birds that we still refer to as coots, as for example, the American Coot, a chicken-like bird that acts like a duck. Hunters held onto "coot" as a name for the scoters long after the naturalists began making the common names more precise. The Black Scoter has been known as the Black Coot, Little Gray Coot, and Smutty Coot, or just plain Coot - or Smutty.

The orange bulge (the "golf ball") on the base of the bill inspired a variety of folk names. There are rather prosaic names: Copper-nose, Yellow-nose, and Yellow-bill. And then there are these: Butternose, Black Butterbill, and Black Coot Butterbill. My favorite folk name for the Black Scoter is Punkin-blossom-coot.

Now back specifically to that Black Scoter on the small pond in Newfane. How does a diving sea duck, that likes to socialize with groups of its own kind, end up on a tiny pond in a small village nestled among the glacially worn, forested hills of Newfane? Good question.

Scoters are sometimes seen in the ponds and set-backs along the Connecticut River or in the Retreat Meadows and West River, suggesting that the Connecticut River Valley is sometimes used by these ducks as a flyway. Newfane is not too far off that course. Or perhaps our Black Scoter was going south along the Lake Champlain flyway and for some reason made a right turn, crossing the Green Mountains, spying the peaceful pond at the end of a long flight, and pausing for a short vacation from his travels. Or perhaps I really don't have a clue as to how he ended up in Newfane, but there he was for about a week, delighting the innkeepers, Newfane residents, and birders who got the word in time for a quick trip to the village.

And then what happened? Again, who knows? Perhaps he was weak, or injured in some way and vulnerable to a fox, coyote, or good sized tomcat. He appeared healthy when I saw him, but appearances do not always tell the whole story. Or maybe he was perfectly fine, rested for those few days, and then resumed his travels to the coast. He found the West River Valley headed southeast to the Connecticut River and then south to Long Island Sound where he reconnected with others of his species. This latter scenario illustrates a genetic lesson about ducks.

In general, there is very little variation among duck species. Populations of songbirds become separated and isolated and develop subspecies. But duck populations are constantly being remixed so that the gene pool remains uniform. A Mallard, Gadwall, or Northern Pintail in Europe is indistinguishable from the same species in North America. Our Black Scoter in Newfane may be an example of how the Black Scoter population gets remixed and remains all one scoter. Our bird may have been flying down Lake Champlain with others of his kind who bred in proximity. He became separated, and will join a different group this winter. The important connection he makes will be with females from a different area. When breeding occurs next year, genes from different areas will mix.

I would rather speculate that the Black Scoter was on his way to blend the gene pool than that he became dinner for a fox. Either way, I can speculate - I can use "maybe" and "possibly" - because I am not a scientist. I am a birdwatcher and a writer. I relished the intimate look at the handsome male scoter, and from that I can let my fancy take flight. That's what a bird watching writer is allowed to do.

"Windhover," - American Kestrel (female)

CHAPTER 18

HAWK FOLK NAMES

A neighbor once told me about the time when a hawk tried to take one of his chickens. The hawk had the chicken in its talons, but the chicken was too heavy to be carried off. Eventually the hawk was chased off and after a little prodding, the chicken realized it was still alive and resumed clucking about the yard, apparently none the worse for its close encounter. But what kind of hawk was it? wondered the narrator.

The early farmers of Vermont would probably have called the hawk a chicken hawk, but that would not tell us very much about its identity. "Chicken hawk" was a name given to all three accipiters, plus the Red-shouldered Hawk. The Red-tailed Hawk was known as the "hen hawk." All of these hawks would have been seen as threats to their domestic fowl and summarily shot.

Any of these hawks might pose a threat to a clueless chicken in the yard, though I wonder whether a four ounce male Sharp-shinned would try such a feat very often. Except when feeding young in the nest, hawks do not have to carry off their kill, and are more likely to feed on the spot. Nor does their attack have to kill their prey. A friend once told me about a Cooper's Hawk which took a Blue Jay in his back yard. The hawk began feeding on the jay even as the jay continued to struggle in its talons. Nature is not always pretty.

Chicken hawks aside, I decided to look further at some of the common names and folk names of our northeastern hawks to see what sort of consistency or logic there might be in the names. Very little as you might imagine.

The Northern Goshawk has been known as the "partridge hawk" and "dove hawk," names derived from what people presumed were its preferred prey. Goshawks winter in our area, feeding on Ruffed Grouse (still called "partridge by many), snowshoe hares, and any other prey which they can find and take. It has also been known as the "blue hawk," for the slate-blue color of the back and wings of the adult, and the "big blue darter." "Darter" has been used for all of the accipiters and reflects the sudden, darting nature of their attack. Accipiters are characterized by stubby wings and long tails which allow them to maneuver through the forest in pursuit of their prey - usually birds. The Northern Goshawk is found in the northern forests of North America, Europe and Asia. "Goshawk" derives from Old English and Old Norse and means "goose hawk."

Cooper's Hawk has also been known as "big blue darter." This hawk was first described by Charles Lucien Bonaparte, a nephew of Napoleon I and one of the foremost ornithologists of his time. His *American Ornithology* was the product of eight years in America studying bird life. He named this hawk in honor of William Cooper of New York, who gave him a specimen which he had shot in 1828. Cooper's Hawk has also been known as the "quail hawk" and the "big stub-winged bullet hawk." The latter is cumbersome but descriptive; if you have ever seen a Cooper's Hawk attack the birds at your feeder, you known that it comes in like a bullet. Two of my favorite hawk folk names belong to the Cooper's - privateer (whose origin I can't even guess at) and striker.

The Sharp-shinned Hawk has also been called "pigeon hawk," "small stub-winged bullet hawk" and "little blue darter." "Sharp-shinned" refers to the flattened, thin tarsus or shank, not exactly a feature which helps with field identification.

Buteos have been slighted by folk culture. Except for the occasional taste for a chicken, they have no folk names of interest. Red-shouldered Hawk was sometimes known as winter hawk, a description now more appropriate to the Red-tailed Hawk. The Broad-winged Hawk must have stayed out of sight in the forest, since it has no folk names at all.

The Northern Harrier - from its habit of raiding, or harrying, its prey - used to be known as the Marsh Hawk and has also been known as "bog hawk," "mouse hawk," "frog hawk," and "snake hawk." Would you like to guess where it is found and what it eats? The Osprey, widely distributed around the world, is the "fish hawk." "Osprey" derives from *ossifraga*, bone-breaker, a term most aptly applied to an Old-World marrow-eating vulture which does not resemble the Osprey at all and seems to have nothing at all to do with the bird's diet or habits.

The falcons fair somewhat better in folk names. "Falcon" comes from the Latin for hawk and refers to the hooked (falcate) shape of the claws. The Peregrine Falcon (from the Latin for alien and wandering) is worldwide. For millennia, it has been favored by nobility for falconry, but the plain yeomen who settled in North America gave it plain names. It used to be known as the "duck hawk," and has also been known as "ledge hawk" and "rock hawk" - for its preferred nesting locations - and most aptly, "bullet hawk." The speed and power of its dive is breathtaking.

There is no satisfactory explanation for the derivation of Merlin, another widely distributed falcon. It used to be known as the "pigeon hawk," perhaps because it looks something like a pigeon in flight, or perhaps because of its feeding habits, though it prefers small land birds and shorebirds. It has also been known as the "blue bullet" and the "little corporal." The latter may be a folk acknowledgment of the little corporal who wore the blue uniform and became the Emperor Napoleon.

The American Kestrel, endemic to North America, used to be known as the "sparrow hawk" - a misnomer, since sparrows are rarely a part of its diet. It resembles, and is closely related to, the Eurasian Kestrel, hence its name. "Kestrel" may derive from the Latin *crepitare,* "to rattle or crackle," which presumably is suggestive of the kestrel's call. "Grasshopper hawk" and "mouse hawk" suggest some of the many, but not exclusive, types of food which it hunts. When alarmed, the kestrel utters a loud, rapid, "killy, killy, killy" - hence, it has been known as the "killy hawk."

I am satisfied with the name, American Kestrel, but if the mavens of bird names ever chose to use the folk name, "Windhover," I would rejoice. This small, beautiful, and most delicate of our raptors is a delight to watch on the wing. It hovers in the wind; it glides and swoops with effortless ease. Again it hangs suspended in the air, hovering on long, delicate, pointed wings - like a sprite, a fairy elf, a Tinkerbell out of Peter Pan - then dives to the grass for a mouse, or cricket, or grasshopper.

The folk names of our northeastern hawks typically reflect the negative aspects of people's encounter with them (hen hawk), or what they saw the hawks take as food (quail hawk), or how they took it (striker). Only one folk name seems to capture the beauty and the poetry of the hawk. The American Kestrel is Windhover.

82

Silent Testimony - Mourning Dove feathers

CHAPTER 19

TALE OF THE TAIL FEATHERS

I never saw the feeder bird.

It is late afternoon on a hot summer afternoon, time to sit on the porch with a cool drink, go back through the morning paper, read the magazine that came in the mail, put the feet up. A breeze dissipates the heat. The waning sun plays light through the leaves, creating thousands of variations on the single color green.

Late afternoon is when the birds become active again. They have the good sense to be quiet during the heat of the day. Perhaps in a cool understory thicket, or the dense branches of a pine, or a roost hole in the forest, they rest or nap. If so, they have more sense than I had on this day; I had mown the lawn, shaded only by a straw hat and cooled only by the warm water riding in the cup holder.

Whatever the birds may be doing through the hot mid-day, by late afternoon the birds are busy around the feeders, or gleaning leaves and bark. Hummingbirds work the beebalm, two or three or four hovering among the red blossoms stretched along the stone wall. The resident tyrant has just about given up his exclusive claim to our yard, but he still protects his feeder.

Chickadees come and go one at a time, hurrying in for their seed, hurrying off to pound it open. Likewise the titmice and nuthatches make quick forays. The Purple Finches come in groups, family groups in all likelihood. The year's young still show red on the base of their bills, a sign of their youth.

That young bill on the young Blue Jays has just about disappeared and they are virtually indistinguishable from the adults. The young woodpeckers still show their red cap and diminutive size. All of the young still do some occasional begging. The begging is almost perfunctory, one last chance to prolong youth and postpone personal responsibility.

I can't read with all this activity, so I just sit and enjoy. Then a Cedar Waxwings alights on the honeysuckle just a few feet away, and another pauses on the end of an apple tree branch. I've been trying to get pictures of the waxwings. Now they've come to me and the camera is inside on the kitchen table. I grumble at myself, rise quietly, and go to fetch it. The birds scatter at my movement.

The waxwings hurry back to the branches of the willow before I can return with my camera. These late nesters are a family. The young are still being tended by their parents. A juvenile buzzes close to a perching parent. The parent flycatches from the branch, makes a swooping foray for a bug, returns to another branch, and is quickly joined by the attentive juvenile. None of the birds perch for long; they are often high in the willow branches and, more often than not, hidden by the foliage. But I stalk them from the ground and manage to get a few photographs. One or two are even in focus and can be kept.

When I return to the porch, the newspaper has been disarrayed by the breeze and my cool drink has warmed. I stuff the paper beneath a cushion and decide that a cool drink is just an indulgence. The birds have scarcely paused in their coming and going as I wandered about my yard. Now I just sit, resigned to watching the free entertainment.

Mourning Doves arrive. The doves only raise two young at a time, but they do it over and over through the summer. The succeeding pairs of young seem to be hanging together now. Maybe their parents are here also. Three doves join a Blue Jay on the platform feeder. They all tussle a bit, but apparently (and surprisingly) decide there is enough room and enough food for all. In the dogwood, a couple of jays look on. A few feet away in the apple tree, a dove perches on the end of a branch; two more are deeper in the tree.

I focus my camera on the platform and watch through the viewfinder as the birds move about. I'm waiting for the right arrangement, a cocked head, an interaction. All I can see is the small field of view through the zoomed lens.

Suddenly, the birds on the platform disappear. They have burst into flight. Nothing unusual about that. Birds at a bird feeder are in the open and exposed. They are alert and skittish. The slightest thing can send them scattering. Did I move my foot? Blink too fast?

The birds on the platform fly with whistling wing whirrs. Jays scream. They always do. In the time it takes to lower my camera, all are gone. Doves are disappearing beyond the river, trailed by the jays. By the apple tree, a few white and tan feathers float slowly toward the ground. An angry jay call fades in the distance. All else is silent.

I walk over to the apple tree. Two small clumps of feathers have settled lightly on the grass. Longer feathers, from a wing or tail are nearby. They are the only signs of the sudden drama that I had been present for but had not seen.

What happened?

A different feeder bird has visited my backyard feeders, not for the seeds, but for the birds that come for the seeds. A hawk. A Sharp-shinned or Cooper's Hawk.

Now I speculate: the dove feathers on the grass are evidence of a successful hunt by an adult, female Sharp-shinned Hawk. Both of these accipiters, Sharp-shinned and Cooper's, have short, rounded wings, long tails and long legs; they are forest raptors with the speed and agility to pursue prey through the trees. The Sharpie is the more common of these two and so the more likely. The female Sharp-shinned is a third to half again as big as the male; she is more likely to have the strength to take and carry off a larger bird, like a dove. The male Sharpie is about the same size and weight as a dove.

Through late summer and fall, I see young Sharp-shinned Hawks quite regularly. They often perch in a tree, watching the feeders. When the jays detect the hawk's presence, the jays loudly mob the hawk, often driving it off. The young Sharpie is clumsy in its attack, not often successful.

I look again at the dove feathers on the grass. There was nothing clumsy about the hawk that took this dove. She was an experienced and adept hunter. I speculate even more: this hawk did not pause in any tree branch to plan its strike. Cruising nearby, perhaps among the trees in the neighbor's yard, or thirty yards overhead, she saw a dove on an exposed branch. With reflex reaction, her long tail ruddered a new direction; she tucked her wings. In less time than the electrical impulses could register danger and transmit the message to flee, she was there and gone with food for herself and perhaps her still dependent young.

I never saw this feeder bird. With my vision obscured by a camera, I did not even have a peripheral impression, a sense of flashing presence. The doves and jays on the platform and in the trees had burst into panicked flight. I knew that now. The dove feathers had settled quietly on the grass, their disarray the only remaining evidence that a hawk had hunted successfully and that the dove had fulfilled its purpose in nature's food chain. Only the scattered wing and tail feathers told the tale.

Golden-crowned Kinglet

CHAPTER 20

KINGLET VERSES WINTER'S WORST

In the nineteenth century, German biologist Carl Bergmann theorized that animals which live in the far north are larger than animals that live to the south. Their larger size enables them to better conserve heat against the cold northern winters. Animals living to the south do not have the same heat conserving need, so they can be smaller. His theory became known as Bergmann's Rule.

The "Rule" makes sense, and we might readily think of the Wooly Mammoth, once the largest mammal to walk the earth and a creature of the frozen edges of the glaciers. The Kodiak bears of Alaska are the largest bears, and polar bears are not far behind. The moose, the largest deer, lives in the northern forest. The largest falcon is the Gyrfalcon and the largest owls are the Snowy and Great Gray Owls, all creatures of the arctic tundra or boreal forests. The largest songbird is the Common Raven, and the largest individuals of this species are those which live in the northern forests.

Unfortunately, the "Rule" is quickly subject to exceptions. North America's largest land bird, the Wild Turkey, ranges south of the Canadian border. The smallest representatives of the grouse family, the White-tailed, Willow, and Rock Ptarmigans are year-round birds of the boreal forest or arctic tundra. And those large predators, the falcon and owls, depend upon the year-round activity of a very small mammal - the meadow vole.

The meadow vole renders Bergmann's rule moot. The final blow is delivered by the Golden-crowned Kinglet. The Golden-crowned Kinglet is the world smallest perching bird. It weighs about two tenths of an ounce (6 grams). It is so small that it has little to fear from most predators; the effort to catch it does not pay enough calory dividends. This kinglet nests in the boreal forests, and some spend the entire year there. Those that wander south in search of food are usually found in the higher elevations and colder habitats of spruce and pine forests.

Golden-crowned Kinglets can be seen, or more likely heard, in our forests throughout the year. In winter, they may be foraging through any coniferous stand. In summer, they are usually in the conifers of higher elevations.

Most of our year round birds are feeder birds. Chickadees, nuthatches, titmice, various finches, and wintering sparrows frequent backyard feeders where they can get the high energy food they need. My feeders seem especially active when a storm is pending, or the temperatures are very low.

But a few birds do not make the seasonal shift to a vegetarian diet. You do not see the Golden-crowned Kinglet at your bird feeder. Nor do you see the Brown Creeper. You might see the latter working a nearby tree trunk, and you might hear or see the kinglet in nearby pine trees. Both stay with an insect-based diet throughout the year.

Go for a walk on the coldest day of the year. Every so often, uncover your ears and listen for a high, thin, buzzy, "zree" or "zee-zee-zee." Then start looking carefully. These tiny, olive colored birds move quickly through the pines and spruces, fluttering wings, hanging upside down as they look for something in the pines and spruces to sustain them. If you are lucky, one may stay put long enough for you to focus your binoculars, if you have them along and can figure out how to keep them from fogging up when brought to your eyes and near your warm breath. If you are really lucky, you may even see the gold crest on top of the head. But the kinglets are too busy in their urgent task to linger more than a moment before moving on.

Bernd Heinrich, University of Vermont biologist, was curious about what the kinglets were eating. In *Winter World* (2003), he describes his pursuit of the kinglet and its food in Maine and Vermont woods over several winters. Analyzing the contents of the kinglet's gizzard, he discovered that they were eating "inchworm" caterpillars. Caterpillars wintering on trees had been unknown. It took him several years to find the caterpillars and then to raise them to the "well-known, one-spotted variant moth (*Hypagyrtis unipunctata*)." Heinrich's persistence discovered the principal winter food source of the Golden-crowned Kinglet, and that a particular moth larvae winters on tree branches and not - like similar species - deep underground where frost does not penetrate.

The winter survival adaptation of the kinglet is directly connected to the winter survival adaptation of the moth larvae on which it feeds. The kinglet is further aided by its bulky, insulating feathers, and by its habit of foraging from first light to last light and then settling beneath nearby protective brush and huddling for warmth.

The kinglet can survive night temperatures of -40F, but it is always close to the edge. A severe winter storm can prove fatal. Heinrich concludes that the kinglet "has no magic key for survival in the cold winter world of snow and ice. Those that live there are lucky and do every little thing right. The odds of surviving the winter are slim ...."

And yet, the kinglet population holds its own, unlike so many species whose numbers are under stress. The kinglet begins nesting in early April, when weather in the northern forests can still be a very dicey and icey. Most songbirds in New England lay four to five eggs. In its tiny, insulated nest hung beneath the protection of evergreen branches, the kinglet lays eight to eleven eggs in a double layer.

A few years ago, amateur ornithologists in Minnesota discovered another secret to the survival of the kinglet. And that is, that while the male is busy feeding the young nestlings, the female is incubating a second clutch with just as many eggs. These very busy parents successfully fledge eighty percent of their young.

The diminutive Golden-crowned Kinglet experiences heavy mortality every winter; it survives by replacing its lost population every summer.

Mother Nature is a harsh parent. There is no benign sentiment. Primitive peoples recognized the forces of nature as forces to be placated. The forces were not tame, and seldom benevolent. When we watch our feeders from the warm comfort of our homes, we are still watching the struggle to survive against those forces. Some birds are perhaps experiencing some benevolence they have not previously known - benevolence in the abundant seed we are providing. But they still must do everything exactly right, and then be lucky.

And yet, for all the starkness, and struggle, we see through our windows, there is life. Beneath the snow pack, there are tunnels and roads made by the voles. On a warm winter day, the birds burst into song and the bees fly. As impending Spring brings the thaw, the snow drops blossom, and bloom follows bloom. Mother Nature may not be

91

benevolent, but she has an irresistible urge to life.

The winter landscape may often seem bleak and lifeless. But moving through the dormant green pine boughs, the kinglet calls "zee-zee-zee." It is talking with its own about food, and the next stop, and shelter. And perhaps also, it is talking to us about life waiting to happen.

Bicknell's Thrush

CHAPTER 21

VERMONT'S ELUSIVE BICKNELL'S THRUSH

Sometimes a bird is talked about with great familiarity, but is rarely seen or encountered. In Vermont, the Bicknell's Thrush is such a bird. I would surmise that most people with some awareness of our Vermont ecology know that the Bicknell's Thrush breeds on some mountain tops and that it is an endangered species. Due very much to the research efforts of the biologists at Vermont Center for Ecostudies, and its success in communicating this research through popular publications and public programs, there is a surprising amount of public awareness concerning this species.

There are two contradictory results for bird watchers. On the one hand, because the Bicknell's Thrush is rare and endangered, some assume that it is impossible to see. On the other hand, because it is so often talked about, others assume that adding the bird to their life list is just a matter of being in Vermont. I had an e-mail from a birder living several states to our south who wanted to make a weekend trip to Vermont to see the Bicknell's. Here are some of the challenges he may face.

The Bicknell's Thrush is only here during the breeding season, roughly a three month period. It is a secretive bird that forages near the ground in thick cover. Under the best of circumstances, it is difficult to see. Even Pete Dunne, in his *Essential Field Guide Companion* has to qualify his description of its feeding habits: "Reported to be fairly nimble and a rapid feeder - mixing short bouts of springy hops with short flights."

The Bicknell's secretiveness is lessened when he is trying to attract the attentions of a female. Then he sings. From late May to early July his song may be heard - at dusk and at dawn. When the light begins to fade, he begins to sing. When the light begins to return in the early hours of a summer morning, he begins to sing. I have been in his habitat at 9 pm, when I heard the first notes of his song, leaving only a few minutes to look for him before stumbling back along the darkened trail. And I have been in his habitat at 8 am on a sunny day when he fell silent, and most recently on a dark and drizzly day at 9am when he offered a few last notes.

Then there is the habitat. Bicknell's Thrush nests in boreal forest with young balsam fir mixed with some spruce and birch. In Vermont, such forest is found at elevations above 3000 feet. Some of these mountain tops are easy to reach in the winter time, when ski lifts are running. But in winter the thrushes are long gone to their tropical homes in the Caribbean.

For all of our second-hand familiarity with Bicknell's Thrush here in New England, acquiring a first hand acquaintance requires planning, effort, at least one good ear for thrush songs, and the usual good dose of luck.

One Saturday in early June, four of us hiked to the top of Stratton Mountain from Kelly Stand Road. We began at 6:15 am. The three and a half miles to the summit is often strenuous, and given our mature years, we were not jogging the route. Along the way we also had to pause for birds best found at higher elevations, such as Yellow-bellied Flycatcher and Blackpoll Warbler. When we reached the top just before 9 am, it was clouded in - damp and misty - with mysterious ribbons of gray floating over and among the trees. A lone White-throated Sparrow sang, but without much enthusiasm.

From just down the trail we heard a loud "Veerrr" - the call of the Bicknell's. At intervals, we heard the call repeated. From somewhere in the tangle a thrush sang - a thin, wiry flute song, notes descending the scale. A bird flashed low across the open trail, and shortly we heard the "Veerrr." The flash of flight was the Bicknell's Thrush. Probably. It was smaller than a robin and did not fly like a robin. We were not hearing Swainson's Thrush. The high elevation warblers would have been in the treetops - and smaller. It was bigger than the sparrows. It was (probably) the Bicknell's. We counted our quest successful.

I had a similar successful quest for the Bicknell's on a June evening on Mt. Equinox several years ago, and a second occasion when one paused briefly on a log beneath dark cover. One year on Stratton Mountain, late during the breeding season, I heard the Bicknell's call and had a distant glimpse. Last year, when surveying for the breeding bird atlas, we continued through our survey area to the top of Stratton when a Bicknell's Thrush paused on an open branch and allowed us to observe him at some leisure.

Memory plays tricks, but I think a research team member once told me that he seldom saw the Bicknell's Thrush except when they were caught in the mist nets for banding and study. It is a very elusive bird and difficult to see.

Having related these cautionary tales about how difficult it can be for most of us to get a really good look at the Bicknell's Thrush, I should probably end this column now. But I can't.

For the Vermont Breeding Bird Atlas project, I surveyed the top of Mt. Snow. Ski trails crisscrossed through the boreal forest on the mountain top before plunging downward. In my four wheel drive pickup, I drove the rugged service road to the summit. We arrived at 5:30 am. The eastern sky was golden, and the sun was just touching the tops of the trees. There were scattered patches of frost. Morning fog lay in many of the stream valleys far below us.

A thrush sang - thin, wiry, descending. We turned toward the thick island of balsam fir where the song had come from. We agreed that there was little chance of seeing the bird in the dense tangle, but we moved slowly toward the edges anyway.

A dark silhouette perched atop a fir, its beak pointed upward to the golden sky - and we heard again the thin, wiry, descending flute-like song. A Bicknell's Thrush proclaimed his territory, and boasted his thrush-ness from the exposed tip.

We wandered about the mountain top listing the species that are drawn to such high elevations for their nesting. Blackpolls were foraging and singing. Purple Finches were displaying. Yellow-rumped Warblers were building nests. And thrushes sang - robins, an occasional Swainson's Thrush, and at one point, at least four Bicknell's Thrushes.

By 8 am, the sun had burned most of the fog out of the valleys and melted the frost. We agreed that the Bicknell's were through singing for the morning ... but what did we know. Thin, wiry, descending notes came from the end of a balsam branch. A Bicknell's Thrush stood on the exposed perch, glowing olive-brown in the early morning sun - unaware of his rare and endangered status - intent and alert only for a mate.

House Wren & Black-capped Chickadee

CHAPTER 22

A NEIGHBORHOOD DISPUTE

There has been a dispute this Spring about housing in our neighborhood, and my spouse and I have been arrayed on opposite sides. For several weeks I thought the housing dispute was going to remain unresolved and our spousal disagreement unreconciled. Ah, but fortunately, that is not the case. The disputing parties have reached an accommodation which makes the disputing parties happy and all parties in my home content.

It all has to do with who constitutes a suitable tenant in our bird houses. We have about a half dozen scattered about our yard; they are well suited to small, cavity nesting birds. For the last several years, at least one of these houses has been home to a Black-capped Chickadee family.

I am partial to the chickadees. They are year round residents providing twelve months of spirited entertainment around my home.

They don't head south with the first sign of a chill in the air. Unlike so many other creatures we see in the summer, Vermont is their four season home. When others are long gone to warmer climes, these hardy little birds are gathering in small groups, foraging through the woods, visiting the feeders, and chattering their "chick-a-dee-dee-dee" chatter, telling their friends about food sources and dangers and going about the task of making a living with enthusiasm and cheer. Even on the coldest winter days and through the foulest of winter storms, they make their hurried visits to the bird feeders with a joie de vivre, always choosing the sunflower seeds, expending that extra energy needed to drill through the outer cover to the choicer, tastier seed within. I've got to like a creature which will choose prime steak over cheap hamburger every time, even when weather conditions suggest just grabbing something fast and easy.

Then comes the Spring, and the chickadees are among the first to turn their thoughts - joyfully and vigorously to - sex. By early April, when the ground is barely free of snow, they are pairing up. Both birds build the nest.

While building the nest, the male defends his territory and chases off potential rivals. The female, on the other hand, is cuckolding her mate at every opportunity. Both birds are very attentive about tending the young of the nest, but alas, the poor male - probably half of the young he is tending were sired by other males. Monogamous pairing among song birds usually relates to the raising of the young. The female gathers as much genetic diversity for her brood as she can manage whenever her mate's back is turned.

Again this Spring I watched their activities. In late April I peeked into the bird house hanging on an old lilac bush. It contained a neat little nest furnished with mosses, plant down, fibers, hair, wool, feathers and spider cocoons, a gentle bed for the 6-8 small eggs which I expected the female to lay soon.

And then on an early morning in early May, I heard my spouse mumble through my half sleep. "Oh wonderful! I just heard the wren." And yes, as I gained consciousness, I heard the long, fast, jumbled, bubbling notes of the House Wren.

When we lived in Pennsylvania, House Wrens nested in our yard. All through May, June and July, we listened to their lively, incessant song - from early morning until dark. Wrens do everything with excessive energy, always flying fast, turning quickly, singing with every feather aflutter. One might almost think they were trying to shame us - don't just sit there! - get busy! - get busy! If you can ignore their implied rebuke, they are a happy sound of summer, no doubt about it. That is why I enjoyed having them nest in our Pennsylvania yard, and it is why my spouse still enjoys having them around our home now.

I would agree with her - except, that House Wrens are aggressive toward other cavity nesting birds, driving other birds from their nests and peremptorily taking over the nest. In his effort to attract a mate, the male builds several sloppy nests. The female may eventually choose one of his nests, finishing it off with an incredible variety of debris.

The House Wren appears around our home every May, but rarely stays. This year he stayed. He enticed a female to join him and set up housekeeping - at the expense of the chickadees. The chickadee nest which I found in late April went unused. The chickadees were driven off by the aggressive wrens.

My spouse was happy to have the wrens. But given a choice, I prefer the chickadees. They stick with me all year. Our differences were irreconcilable. Then one day in late May, she came in from gardening to tell me that chickadees were around another nest box, as though they might be making a nest. Two days later, I saw the wren on top of that box bubbling and chattering away. The chickadees were gone.

In early June I walked near yet another bird house and saw a chickadee poke his head out of the gap between the roof and the side. Would he be evicted again by the domineering wren. Not this time. But it wasn't the chickadee becoming impervious to the bullying of the wren. The wren was otherwise occupied. On the other side of our yard, a nest box hung from the branch of an ash tree. Here the female wren had finally made a nest out of the mess which the male had started. And from within, I could here the buzzy demands of young for food. The wren parents were busy feeding their hatchlings and simply did not have time to police their neighborhood against the darn locals who wanted to live there too.

So, as of the middle of this week, there has been no resolution in the conflict between the year round and the seasonal residents, but there is an accommodation. The wrens are still bubbling their notes with every foray for food, but they are way too busy to patrol the neighborhood. The chickadees are patiently - and quietly - incubating. And inside our home, both of us are happy - each of us has our favorite bird nesting in our yard.

A stovepipe keeps squirrels off the feeder, but Blue Jays scatter seeds to the ground

CHAPTER 23

HOW TO KEEP SQUIRRELS OUT OF BIRD FEEDERS

A woman approached me one Sunday after church. Agitated, she asked: "What can I do to keep the squirrels away from my bird feeder? They just clean me out."

I responded, "You can't do anything. They're smarter than you are."

She asked, "What about one of those squirrel proof feeders?"

I answered, "There is no such thing. The squirrels are smarter than the engineers."

Anyone who has watched squirrels find their way to a bird feeder, knows that I was not being flippant. Squirrels are capable of overcoming the most ingenious obstacles devised by humankind. Their feats are legendary. They are not only leaping acrobats, tumbling gymnasts, and Spiderman scalers, but they seem to have a problem-solving and reasoning ability. There is no way to guarantee that all squirrels can be kept out of all feeders all the time.

I was given a bird feeder with a lever that automatically closes the seed access when weighted by a sitting squirrel. It works when the gray squirrel sits on the lever, but not when the squirrel hangs upside down from the roof. The squirrel rarely does that because it cannot get enough seed out of the narrow opening. It can get more seed faster from cleaning up the ground than from stealing from this feeder. Unfortunately, the birds do not care for the feeder either. Only one or two birds can visit this feeder at one time. Since I like lots of bird activity, this (semi) squirrel-proof feeder will never be my only feeder.

The large tubular feeder has two rows of perches. The perches and feeder openings are all metal. The feeder is atop a metal pole and is protected top and bottom by a squirrel baffle. Squirrels are able to defeat the baffles and cling to the perches, but so far they have not been able to gnaw through the metal or get their teeth started on the plastic tube. My supply of sunflower seeds has not been diminished by the squirrels. The birds love this feeder. It is not uncommon to have all sixteen perches on the two levels occupied in a maelstrom of feeding frenzy. Unfortunately, the feeder is only good for the smaller birds. Larger birds like the cardinal, grosbeaks, jays and doves are unable to get seeds from the small openings. I cannot exclude some of my favorite birds just because of the squirrels, so this feeder cannot be the only one.

I put suet in a wire metal basket. The woodpeckers and songbirds can feed through the wire mesh, but the squirrels can only gnaw at the suet when it has been packed tight after filling. As sharp as their teeth are, they have not yet evolved a wire-cutting edge. However, I have watched a red squirrel lift the top of the suet feeder and chew off the top portions of the suet. This was almost enough to make me into a gun owner, although my firing of a .22 would probably pose more danger to the birds, the neighbor's dog and my indoor cats than it would to the red squirrel.

I once read that the solution to squirrels and bird feeders is to place the bird feeder at least twelve feet from anything that the squirrel can climb up and jump from. I have had some success with this plan. I placed a large feeder (it holds about 15 pounds of seed) on a 4x4 post. For a baffle, I used a three foot section of 6 inch stove pipe suspended by two nails. This worked quite well. One squirrel occasionally reached the feeder by running rapidly up the two foot section of the post not protected by the stove pipe and leaping to the feeder. But this squirrel was not always successful in the leap, and only attempted the leap when the ground seed was covered by snow.

However, the placement of a feeder in the open creates a problem for the birds. Songbirds like cover close by to which they can flee when a predator comes near. A feeder set in the open twelve feet from any trees or shrubs does not provide cover. So I planted a red-twig dogwood nearby, and for a few years it provided some of the needed cover. However, the wood shrub is now as high as the eaves and easily supports the weight of a squirrel. It was like providing the squirrel with stairway access to the food stores. The big gray rodent sat on the feeder, defiantly facing my kitchen window, and stuffed its cheeks full of my bird seed. Fifteen pounds of seed could disappear in a couple of days.

I finally had enough of that, and moved the post feeder with the stovepipe baffle to the middle of the yard, carefully measuring with my tape rule a spot at least twelve feet from the nearest thin branch of the apple tree. The post is close to low quince and scrub roses, so there is cover for ground feeding sparrows. The feeder is angled so that the back faces the large trees from which hawks might hunt, thus providing some protection to the feeder birds. So far it has worked. Squirrels have been around assessing the situation, but have not yet breached my defenses.

This means that when I fill this feeder with fifteen pounds of seed, it takes a long time for the birds to empty the feeder. I wish! Yesterday

I watched three Blue Jays shoveling the seed onto the ground, picking one seed to eat, then shoveling more seed. This was not new; I've seen this happen before. I used to consider this a symbiosis whereby the small ground-feeding birds watched for hawks while the Blue Jays were scattering seed on the ground.

But now I'm not so sure. As the jays were shoveling seed to the ground, a squirrel was there stuffing the scattered seed into its cheeks. Paranoia kicked in. Could those jays be in league with the squirrels? Have the squirrels hired the jays to shovel seed for them? Is there a nefarious contract between the jays and the squirrels? How much are the squirrels paying the jays to shovel the seed? Can I subpoena bank records to find out? Is there a lawyer who can tell if I have probable cause? Please can someone tell me how I can keep the squirrels from eating my bird seed?

Black-throated Sparrow

CHAPTER 24

THE LIFE LIST HITS A MILESTONE

I am a birding hobbyist. Not an ornithologist. Not a guru of birding excursions, instantly knowing every bird which happens through my line of sight. I bird because I am fascinated by these feathered creatures, lured by their beauty, awed by their grace.

I am also a life lister. I keep a record of the birds I have seen. So that you know that I am not totally obsessed, I only keep track of the birds I have seen in North America. When traveling outside of our continent, I have given only passing attention to the birds. I caution my long-suffering spouse to keep me that way if she can.

I am an active life lister. My spouse, by contrast, is a casual life lister. She says, "Is that a new bird for me?" I say, "That's a new bird!" In the emotions of birding, there is a big difference.

Life listing is typically testosterone related - males are more likely to be active life listers than females. It is a bloodless way of sorting out the best hunters, counting coup without danger, collecting heads without paying a taxidermist and hanging them on the wall. It is like the helmets of high school football players emblazoned with stickers for their outstanding play. It is scars on the body, but without the scars. The life list is the birding equivalent of those ugly little statues in the trophy case. Ah, but you get the point I am sure - the life list is the mark of the serious birder, the accomplished birder, or at least, of the birder who can count.

I came late to serious life listing. When I moved to Vermont eight years ago, my life list was in the fairly modest 350 range, having been helped by several western vacations in the mid-80s. One aim of my move was to reorder my life so that I could find time for my non-vocational interests, one of those interests being birding. The first winter I went to Plum Island with local birders; the trip produced five new birds for my life list, and ever since the list has been creeping slowly upward. I hit 400 with the White Ibis on a trip four years ago to southern Texas and the Rio Grande, got additional boosts on subsequent trips to Florida and California, and have picked up scatterings here and there in the northeast.

At the beginning of this year, my life list was 491. Our winter birding trip was to southeastern Arizona, a vagrant trap, and an extension of Mexican habitat north of the border. Species which can be found no where else in North America, show up in southeastern Arizona regularly. A few even make the area their permanent home. Plus, it was a place and habitat that I had never been to before, which meant birds I had never before had the opportunity to see. I was primed! I was ready! I would hit 500!

Did I? You bet! It took until the second day, but I hit the 500 milestone, and kept on going!

On the first day outside of Tucson, we began our birding at

Sweetwater Ponds. Development in the desert southwest has dried up most natural wetlands, but municipalities have created new ones in the process of treating their waste water. Tucson has done an especially commendable job, creating habitat and parkland. The ponds were full of Northern Shovelers, Cinnamon Teals, and Ruddy Ducks with males in breeding plumage and sporting their oddly colored blue beaks. Within the first few steps, Gambel's Quail appeared along the pathway, Abert's Towhee flew between bushes, and a Verdin fed on a scrubby tree. Heading into the Sonoran Desert, we picked up Gilded Flicker and Gila Woodpeckers contesting nest holes in the Saguaro Cacti, Cactus Wren inserting their noisy opinions, Canyon Towhee going about their business, and Brewer's Sparrows being so nondescript that their very non-description gave away their identity. A casual, get acquainted-with-the-area day of birding produced over sixty species, eight life birds, and a life list which stood at 499.

The next day in the desert outside of Willcox, the group we were with studied a huge flock of sparrows. Brewer's and White-crowned Sparrows dominated, but there were also lots of winter plumage Lark Buntings, a scattering of Versper Sparrows, some Chipping Sparrows and one or two Black-throated Sparrows. Finally the Black-throated Sparrows stayed still long enough to get a clear look, a definitive look. Number 500 on my life list.

The ticks continued from there: Mexican Jay (found only in southern Arizona mountains), Mexican Chickadee (found only at high elevations in the Chiricahua Mountains), southern Arizona specialties like the Yellow-eyed Junco, Red-naped Sapsucker, Arizona Woodpecker, common and uncommon western species such as the Lesser Goldfinch, Lawrence's Goldfinch, Black-chinned Sparrow, and Sage Sparrow. Southern Arizona is famous for its hummingbirds, attracting tropical hummingbirds found no where else north of the border. Only a few are hardy enough to winter over, but we got them: Blue-throated Hummingbird and Magnificent Hummingbird.

On our final day, and our last stop, we returned to the Sonora Desert Museum outside of Tucson, to see a few exhibits we had missed earlier and to visit the gift shop. But I froze on the walkway, and whispered urgently to my spouse: "Costa's Hummingbird." A male Costa's perched atop the dried seed pods of a desert plant, its purple crown and long flared throat feathers iridescent even in the dull light of the overcast afternoon. It was the last bird we listed on our trip. It was a great way to end a week of Good Birding! And it was number 516 on my life list. But who's counting?

Bufflehead

CHAPTER 25

SEX IN WINTER

I am not much for television. I prefer spending my idle time with a good book - or even a bad one. But once in a while, I feel that I should try to connect with the dominate culture around me. The Super Bowl provides me with the excuse to do that. Generally speaking, I am appalled. The mega-hype is so mega-skewed from reality. One would think that the end times of the Apocalypse were about to occur, rather than a usually boring, typically mediocre football game. The pre-game and half-time entertainment leaves me wondering why anyone else in the world would want to be like us; it is so mega-tasteless, even without the occasional costume accident - and boring.

And then there are the commercials. There have been Super Bowls in the past when the only real entertainment was provided by the commercials. Recently, they have simply been inane and bad? Is this what the big corporations really think about the intellectual level of the

American male? If so, that may also explain why so many of the commercials are based on the same theme: sex. Any man who buys razor blades, muscle SUVs, or beer because he thinks, per the commercials, that he will get sex, probably is only getting it in the fantasy of the commercial. It is enough to drive one to drink.

So ... what is it that has set off this minor rant on the fantasy sex lives of American males as they bulk up with beer and pizza? Birds, of course. While many men seem to be dreaming about sex in the winter, there are birds that are proactively interacting with the opposite sex in the pursuit of sex. Rather than suppressing the sex drive beneath layers of clothing and bedding or retreating to the fantasy of a razor blade, a few species use the winter months to form their pair bonds, regardless of any frigid winter temperatures.

Winter is when many male ducks are at their most spectacular. They are in their finest plumage, decked out to impress females with their superior genes. Along the Massachusetts coast in wintertime, I love to watch drake Buffleheads as they gather around one or two hens. Their black and white plumage glitters in the cold air; their hoods are raised as they splash on the water's surface.

I don't have to go to the coast for the courting display of waterfowl. Several species gather in the open water of the Connecticut River below the Vernon dam. In mid-winter they are busily engaged in courtship. A short way below the dam is an exposed rock. It is a favorite place for the wintering Common Goldeneyes. A flock of forty to sixty goldeneyes often congregate there - the number is difficult to estimate because they are diving ducks, and a significant number, at any one time, are underwater looking for food. They can be seen with the naked eye, but to see their display binoculars are needed, or better yet, a scope.

The male Common Goldeneyes are resplendent in their breeding plumage - or perhaps more correctly - in their courting plumage. By the time actual breeding takes place much to the north, pair bonds will have been formed, and the male's plumage will have become worn and ragged.

Do be careful not to confuse the Common Goldeneye with the Common Merganser. Both can be found below the Vernon dam, and both show a large amount of white on their sides. The mergansers are usually some distance from the goldeneyes, and like the rougher currents closer to the dam. They have long narrow, orange bills. The male's head is entirely green, without the white spot characteristic of the goldeneye.

In his courtship, the male goldeneye "swims about the female, often with head lowered and neck stretched along the water, but his most characteristic motion is that of raising his head upward and backward until, with the bill pointing toward the zenith, he utters his harsh note. Sometimes the head is thrown over until it almost touches the back. Often the bird dashes forward while the orange-colored feet strike backward and upward with such force as to throw strong jets of water into the air and at the same time display the brilliant coloring." (Forbush)

The stretching of the neck and throwing it upward and backward happens with such force that it makes me fearful of whiplash, but apparently it is impressive to the females. It is also noticeable, even at the distance.

If you have a scope, and are patient, perseverant, and lucky, you may also see a Barrow's Goldeneye among the flock of Common Goldeneyes. The Barrow's is much less common than the Common; because of its rarity, its presence is always noted by active birders. The drake Barrow's in breeding plumage is marked by less white on the side and a line of clear white spots along the wing - rather than the thin streaks of black on white wings sported by the Common. There may also be a female Barrow's Goldeneye below the dam, but the distance is too great to distinguish her subtle differences from the female Common Goldeneyes, at least so far. The two species are closely related and occasionally interbreed. The drake Barrow's Goldeneye is busily engaged in courtship display along with the drake Commons.

Also courting below the dam in smaller numbers is the Hooded Merganser. The males are in their plumaged glory and when displaying raise their hammerhead crest with its large white patch. Their orange sides will distinguish them from the Bufflehead which has a similar white crest and sometimes winters on the river or shows up early in the Spring.

Owls begin courting and nesting in early February, although you may have to be out late at night to hear them. And other birds may be at it as well. A friend e-mailed me early one February and described a pair of Pileated Woodpeckers doing "a sort of dance around our trees. They went from tree to tree in the woods on the periphery of our yard, circling each tree, gently pecking at the trunk and gently sparing with their bills. They remained one or two feet above the snow line on each tree, spending a few minutes on each one before moving on to another."

While some sedentary America males are quaffing beer and fantasizing, some of our birds are actively pursing sex in the winter.

Blackpoll Warbler - boreal & mountain top nester

CHAPTER 26

ON THE TRAIL TO STRATTON MOUNTAIN

Tom is a section hiker of the Appalachian Trail. For several years, he has left the comfort of his home in Indiana and spent about five weeks hiking the trail. This year he began in Connecticut and continued the route north. Much of the time, he had to contend with daily rains turning the trail into a quagmire and making meals and nights a challenge.

But on this day the weather was clear and the early morning temperature pleasant. The sun had quickly burned the fog out of the valleys and had nearly cleared the summit of Mt. Stratton. Tom came slowly up the trail to where we were standing. We were somewhere below the summit, standing still, listening and looking, binoculars ready.

We greeted each other. "Bird watching?" he asked us. "What are you seeing?"

Often the question is a polite one, on the order of "How's it going?"

A perfunctory response such as, "Not much" or "Just a couple of common warblers" satisfies the one asking and sends all of us on our way.

But Tom persisted and so we named the warblers we were hearing and occasionally seeing as we stood in the middle of the trail: Black-throated Blue Warbler, Black-throated Green Warbler, Yellow-rumped Warbler. "I only see those as passing migrants in Indiana," he said. A distant Winter Wren sang his jumbled, tumbling musical notes.

He continued to ask about birds. "Any Hooded Warblers?" - "No, we're too far north." - "How about Worm-eating Warblers?" - "Probably not. Again, we're too far north. There's a Blue-headed Vireo singing, another common breeder in our woods." His head tilted as he listened for the song.

Typically, through hikers on the Appalachian Trail scarcely break stride as they hurry past huffing day hikers. Tom wasn't typical. He did not move on. He was a birder, although on the trail he did not carry the extra weight of binoculars. He told us, "You're the first birders I've met this year."

With frequent interruptions as we paused to listen or to lift our binoculars toward some tree top movement, we told him that we were volunteers working on the Vermont Breeding Bird Atlas. We were working a five kilometer square that included Little Stratton, but did not extend to the summit of Mt. Stratton. This section of our block was accessible only by first walking two miles. We needed to do this because the elevation reached over 3000 feet and provided habitat for species that could not be found at lower elevations.

A high thin series of "zi" notes provided an illustration, and we drew his attention to a Blackpoll Warbler, one of the spruce forest species we needed to document.

Tom asked about thrushes. On cue, a Hermit Thrush sang. During our early morning walk, we had also heard the Wood Thrush and the Swainson's Thrush. At three thousand feet we were hoping for a Bicknell's Thrush. His eyes showed a glint of extra interest. We went on to explain that they nested on the top of Mt. Stratton where biologist had been studying them since they were "split" from the Gray-cheeked Thrush and became a species in their own right, and an endangered species. We were hoping to find the Bicknell's Thrush in the Little Stratton area. One of our group of three said she hoped to see the Bicknell's, period. It would be a new bird for her.

As we started to move along, we stepped aside so that Tom could go ahead and not be slowed by our stop-listen-look pace. He led, but every time we paused, he paused. After a bit, he explained that the twenty-something hikers race along, covering twenty-five or more miles a day, never pausing to look at anything. "I can't see the sense to that."

When a Yellow-bellied Flycatcher sang his "chebunk" from a thick stand of spruce, he stood among us, so that four pairs of eyes searched for some movement that would give away the location.

And then, as we moved into forest where dense, shrubby spruce began to dominate, we heard a breathy, nasally thrush song, and all went on full alert. Tom was a few paces ahead with one of our group. "There! On the branch!" Binoculars pointed up. The bird sang. Tom was handed a pair of binoculars and he watched the Bicknell's Thrush as it sang again. It moved to another branch: a brownish bird, lightly speckled beneath the chin - not a candidate for most beautifully plumaged - but again he sang his flute-like thrush song. On one leg he wore a small red band. He was one of the birds which the biologists were studying.

Another Bicknell's sang. "That's a new bird for me!"

Tom said, "For me too! I can't wait to tell my friend back home. He'll probably jump on a plane and fly out here."

A few more yards along the trail and we were on the summit of Mt.

Stratton. We talked with the caretakers who live on the summit during the summer. We climbed the fire tower, where Tom was able to view where he had been and where he was going. We sat in the shade as the day warmed and ate our lunch. I used to live near the Appalachian Trail in Pennsylvania and volunteered at a hostel for hikers. Tom was a different type of hiker. He was in no hurry to hurry on his way. He absorbed the lore of the trail from the caretakers, relished the thrushes singing from several spruce tops, talked of birding experiences, looked forward to when he could tell his friend about his Bicknell's sighting.

Eventually of course, we had to return south to Kelly Stand Road and Tom had to resume his route going north. Tom's pace probably picked up, since he was running short on food and would soon have to find his way into a town to resupply. Our walk down from Stratton was leisurely, with many stops for further bird listening and bird watching - leisurely also because our older bones were beginning to protest ever so slightly.

The Bicknell's Thrush did not get counted in our survey area, because we were practically to the top of Mt. Stratton, and outside of our survey area when we met up with it. But, we three Vermont birders do not normally see this species, living as we do in the valleys. Additionally, we were able to share our experience with Tom. As we shook hands with Tom on the top of Stratton and parted company with him, he said: "Thanks so much for letting me tag along with you. This has been the highlight of my time on the trail this year."

We had two good encounters on the trail to Stratton - with the Bicknell's Thrush and with an interested and interesting AT hiker. Good birding often means meeting good people and sharing good experiences.

Downy Woodpecker feeding young

CHAPTER 27

THE NEXT GENERATION

Our daughters and their children have been visiting this week. A toddler, almost toddler, and four year old are always into something, asking for something, doing something. By the end of the day when my wife and I have crawled into bed, we were almost too tired to read. Just before the book fell from her hands, she said, "Watching the kids is exhausting" - this from someone who appears to most people to have boundless energy.

Of course, all we need to do to know how much energy kids require of parents (and grandparents) is to watch the neighborhood. There are kids galore making demands on parents. Nestling birds are, or soon will be, leaving the nest, and the trees and bushes are frantic with activity.

In a quiet moment last weekend I watched a male Downy Woodpecker working the branches of the maple tree close to my porch. With his beak full of tasty larvae, he flew through the treetops across the river, heading toward his nest hole. When birds are foraging for themselves, they eat on the spot. But if you see them carrying food, you know that they have a nest somewhere nearby.

The next day, sitting on the porch with four year old Julius, I glimpsed two Downy Woodpeckers fly into the maple. Although they remained hidden by the leaves, their identity had been suggested by flight, call, and posture when they landed. One flew to the suet feeder. "There's Daddy Downy," I told Julius, explaining that the red spot on the back of his head meant this was the daddy. As he flew into the tree carrying suet I explained further. "He is feeding his baby."

The male Downy returned to the suet feeder. A second woodpecker flew to the post of another bird feeder. This one had a red cap on the top of its head, a certain sign that it was a juvenile. The red cap of the juvenile Downy Woodpecker will disappear by the end of summer, but until then a quick glance might make you think you are seeing a Yellow-bellied Sapsucker which has a similar red cap.

To Julius I said, "Look, there's Daddy Downy's baby."

Laughing he said, "Noooo, that's too big to be a baby. He's bigger than his daddy."

In the brief look we had at the juvenile Downy Woodpecker, it certainly looked bigger than its parent. Which - as I tried to explain in four year old terms - is not unusual for baby birds. Young birds are often larger than their parents. Parent birds are adept at finding food and they stuff as much as they can into the gapping maws of their young, even after they have fledged. Soon those young birds will be abandoned by their parents, sent out to make it on their own. They are going to have to forage for themselves. The larger size of the young bird means extra reserves of stored fat to carry them through the lean time until they learn how to find their own food. If they can learn that lesson before the fat reserves are burned up, and are lucky enough to avoid predators, then they may survive.

The ways of the adult world are lessons which all youngsters, even the four year old sitting on my lap, have to learn sooner or later. Thousands of fledglings will soon be learning it for themselves, as evidenced by the frenzied activity everywhere. A month ago, when two birds were in hot pursuit of one another, it was the mating ritual. Now it is most likely a fledgling pursuing a parent in hopes of food. Even at this point, it is still a matter of survival. The most insistent, most aggressive, most demanding of the brood is also most likely to be fed, and thus grow and survive. Many don't.

I watched a Tufted Titmouse family fly into a lilac. The young were still together and close to their parents. But soon they will become scattered. Only a few feet may separate the young siblings, but that may be just enough for one to get the food it needs and the other to be missed.

High pitched buzzing from the tree tops drew my attention to Cedar Waxwings flying in tight pursuit. Somewhat later nesters than many songbirds, I thought at first that I was seeing a courtship flight. Their small brown forms disappeared into the trees. Then on a branch I saw one perched, its wings fluttering rapidly. A young bird was demanding food and a parent obliged. As the adult flew off, the youngster was right on its tail.

White-breasted Nuthatch parent and fledgling have been at the feeders. So have young Common Grackles and young Mourning Doves; the adult Mourning Doves are working on their second brood of the summer. Purple Finches are back at the feeders, the young in fresh, bright plumage.

A noisy crowd of Yellow-bellied Sapsuckers descended on the weeping willow, the parent bringing food while the youngsters practiced their pecking - weak, tentative tapping, but already with the characteristic slowing down that makes this one of the easiest members of the woodpecker family to identify by the drumming.

Julius and I watched Daddy Downy fly to the thin metal post on which the suet feeder hung. We laughed when his feet, designed for gripping tree bark, couldn't hold him on the post. He slid down like a fireman coming down the firehouse pole. He was waiting his turn at the suet. Mama Hairy Woodpecker was gathering food for her youngster who was waiting in the maple with very little patience. As soon as she flew to her fledgling, Daddy Downy took her place on the suet. Ripping off pieces of the nutrition rich food, he flew across the river where another youngster must have been calling. In fast pursuit was the young Downy who had been waiting in the tree, noisily protesting that he had been first in line.

For a few minutes Julius and I were entertained by feathered daddies and mommies and babies. But a four year old has many things to do, and Julius had clean clothes to get dirty and mud pies to make. So I kept an eye on him as he toiled by the river. But I also kept an eye on the sky, watching for the next feathered parents tending their next generation.

Zucchini

CHAPTER 28

ZUCCHINIS DON'T HAVE FEATHERS!

This chapter began as a comment to a posting by my daughter on her blog. As I wrote my comment, I got carried away. Some readers, before they get to the end - if they get that far - may feel I did not get carried far enough away. The principle subject is zucchini - and yes, I know, zucchinis don't have feathers, and this book is supposed to be about living things that have feathers. But hang in - maybe I'll work a bird in sooner or later.

I tell my grandchildren - always listen to your parents. The operative word is "always." But there seems to come a point when children regard the operative word as inoperative.

My oldest thirtysomething daughter who lives in Philadelphia returned home from her vacation in Vermont to find huge zucchinis growing in her garden. She wrote about it on her blog. While she was unpacking, her eight year old son brought in a big zucchini. "Look what

I found, Mom." Then he appeared with another huge zucchini, and another. They kept on coming.

The problem is that zucchini bread doesn't take very much zucchini and other recipes calling for zucchini - while tasty to some - are not liked by everybody (e.g. a five year old granddaughter). And none of the recipes begin to use up a watermelon sized zucchini.

I have often told a story to my family of my experience with zucchini 30 years ago - a story which has been ignored - one which could have avoided the cord of zucchini now accumulating in my daughter's home. All she had to do was ask, "What was that story you told about zucchini?" Or even asked, "You have a garden, dad, do you grow zucchini?"

Always ask your parents advice and listen to your parents, I tell my grandchildren, the children of my daughter. Had my daughter asked her parent, I would have advised - nay, I would have warned - do not grow zucchini.

Thirty years ago I had a small garden. I got a few vegetables from it. Except zucchini! My zucchinis attained the size of watermelons. Everyone who came to the front door had to take a zucchini. We sold an old piece of furniture; the condition of sale was modest - take just one zucchini. It got so the mailman refused to deliver mail until I granted him dispensation.

The stories about zucchini are not hard to come by. I have been told that a few years ago a local farmer harvested his zucchini and sent them to market. He had to hire a logging truck to move the produce. The truck took a curve too fast and spilled the load across Route 9 - the road was closed for two days. The story sounds incredulous, unless you've ever grown zucchini.

Just ask the question, dear daughter, such as, "Dad, do you think growing zucchini is a good idea?" I am older and wiser so I do not plant zucchini. Last year I did not plant any of those type plants (pumpkins, squash, gourds, cukes) because the squash bugs needed to be starved out. This year I did. But not zucchini! I have a bed of summer squash - those ones that produce small, dainty yellow and green fruits. I harvested some yesterday. One of those dainty green squashes was almost the size of a small zucchini. The pile covered my kitchen table. I gave some to the neighbors, and used others for my covered dish contribution to a pot luck dinner. The pile is still growing.

So to my grandchildren - always listen to your parents and ask their advice. Or even better, ask your grandparents - they are even older and wiser and more experienced. You may not need to do this for everything but if you are planting a garden, by all means ask. Your granddad would have given you a severe warning about the dangers of zucchini in the garden.

Some advice to my daughter, even though she hasn't asked - but should: be merciful to your children. Do not visit the sins of the parents upon them. They do not need to eat zucchini for breakfast ... lunch ... dinner ... not even zucchini disguised by your creative and tasty recipes.

Instead, find new ways to use the zucchini - perhaps as speed bumps on the street in front of your home. Maybe the city of Philadelphia could use them as impact barriers at dangerous places along the Schulykill Expressway. Perhaps you could set up a stand in front of the ballpark and sell the smaller ones (football sized) to the Phillies' home crowd; Philadelphia sports fans have a reputation for rowdiness and throwing things on the field. (On the other hand, maybe that's not such a good idea.) Or why not give them to the Pentagon? The Pentagon could then threaten to deliver a plane load of zucchinis to a terrorist enclave. This would be more effective than a lot of the posturing that is done.

A few weeks ago I wrote about the scolding I received from a

House Wren. (Here's the bird I promised.) My daughter - the one who failed to asked advice about zucchini - commented on the column. They live on the edge of one of Philadelphia's steep hills; it is wooded, overgrown, and perfect habitat for a House Wren. Their House Wren, in the House Wren manner, is incessantly noisy. Our oldest grandson, the eight year old, helps his dad in the garden. My daughter wrote, "He gets so fed up with the never-ending harangue from the wrens that he yells, 'Shut up!' They don't listen to him."

Now you might think that this Philadelphia House Wren was merely doing his normal thing - impressing the ladies and warning off rivals. But I don't think that is the case. House Wrens travel widely about the country, from north to south. They see many things, much more than urban dwellers with their narrow, parochial, and asphalt dominated perspectives. I think that House Wren in my daughter's back yard was doing what I was unable to do, because I'm in Vermont and they're in Philadelphia. That House Wren was warning them not to plant zucchini! He'd been around. He knew. But those city dwellers, so isolated from the real world, didn't understand a word he said.

So again I tell my grandchildren - always listen to your parents. And remember the word "always." Or better yet, draw upon real wisdom, - wisdom based on long experience - the wisdom of your venerable grandparents. Had your parents done that, they would have known not to plant zucchini.

With that sage advice, it is now time to go outside and look for birds.

Tufted Titmouse in winter

CHAPTER 29

IN A RACE FOR LIFE

I have written once about the word "cute" as it is applied to birds. In the summer, very young birds are typically described as "cute," although in fact they are clueless. They chase parents around, begging for food. They are slow in learning about food sources, and slower in learning about danger. I took a lot of friendly teasing over my protest on the use of "cute," and probably did not change the verbal habits of anyone, but I shall continue to insist that "cute" is not an appropriate adjective.

Now it is winter, and some of the birds coming to the bird feeders are still "cute" in the minds of many. And some are apparently still clueless. I admit that I enjoy watching the frenetic activity of many of the birds which feed on my largess. Along with my favorite companion (who is likely to use words like "cute" or "adorable") I especially enjoy the woodpeckers, chickadees, titmice, and nuthatches.

The two woodpeckers, the Downy and the Hairy, wait patiently in nearby trees when I take in the suet feeder to refill it. When I rehang the suet feeder, I call out, "Okay, guys, come and get it." There is a bit of chatter and by the time I am back in the kitchen, they are on the suet or waiting a turn on branches overhead. The Hairy is stocky and robust, and doesn't say much to me. The Downy is "cute" as it peers down at me and chatters a "thank you," or perhaps a "couldn't you do it faster next time."

The chickadees, titmice, and nuthatches come quickly to a feeder, grab a seed, and fly. Their acrobatics are entertaining. The actions of these year-round neighborhood residents are not all that different from what the juncos and sparrows are doing, but the ground feeders are not described as "cute" nearly so often.

The secret is in the eyes. The dark eye of the junco is not as noticeable against its dark head as is the dark eye of the titmouse. But any of these birds, or any small songbird, might on some occasion perch on a branch and look down at you with its head turned and cocked to the side, giving you the curious once-over in a very "cute" manner.

But there is serious business in the head-cocking, neck turning, hurry up - grab the seed - head to the bushes. The big eyes are located on the sides of the head, giving them a wide vision as they constantly watch for danger. They turn their head in order to get a look at me. And more importantly, they don't linger to study a sudden movement in the periphery of their vision; they flee.

We call them "bird feeders," but our bird feeders feed much more than just small songbirds. There are red squirrels and gray squirrels which find food on the ground or in the feeders. Field mice run tunnels beneath the snow, and gather the seed. Chipmunks stuff their cheeks throughout the fall and cache the seed in their burrows. At night deer feed on the fallen apples and lick the platform clean of seed. At different times of the year, skunk and bear scavenge food.

There are all kinds of food at the bird feeders. There is seed which feeds birds and animals. And then there are the birds and animals which feed other birds and animals. The eyes of predators do not look to the side. Their two eyes look forward. With keen binocular vision, they look for food. A fox looks for a mouse; a fisher spies a grouse. Your sweet, family cat with its eyes in front, hunts rodents and birds. Stealthily slipping into a tree, the Sharp-shinned or Cooper's Hawk studies the food possibilities around the feeders.

I sit at my kitchen table and watch the birds outside my window. A dozen Blue Jays are going to and from the various feeders. Suddenly they fly ... and every other bird flies; the jays are screaming loudly as they disappear into the pines. Somewhere nearby there is a hawk.

When the jays begin their loud alarm calls, I pay attention. They are warning everyone of danger. On a rare occasion, I see the jays mobbing a still silhouette in a tree, preemptively dealing with danger. A couple of times a year, I see a sudden flash through the yard as a hawk makes its attack. Most often, I see only scattered feathers lying about the grass or fluttering across the snow, silent evidence that the life and death struggle to find food has played out with some birds winning, and others losing in a fatal way.

When you put out a bird feeder, you must accept that hawks will come as well as chickadees. Sharp-shinned and Cooper's Hawks are feeder birds. You can put your feeder where there is cover for the small birds - bushes, pines, trees - the thicker and more tangled, the more protection. But you must accept that hawks are sometimes going to look for food among the birds at your feeders, and sometimes they will be successful. If you cannot accept that, and leave the hawk unmolested as it hunts, kills, and dines, then you have no business feeding the birds.

Beyond those feathers scattered about the yard, I have had two recent experiences which lead me to issue the following: Warning, bird feeders are not for the faint of heart.

On my platform feeder a week ago, a Blue Jay was busy eating. It ate seed after seed after seed. But unlike the other jays, it did not come and go. Feathers around its neck were disordered and messy. One wing did not fold against its body and primary feathers were askew. When it finally flew, it did so with difficulty. In all likelihood, this Blue Jay had a near fatal encounter with something. Perhaps it damaged its wing as it fled from a hawk through a tangle. Perhaps it was hit by a young hawk, still not adept at taking prey, and escaped, but with injury. I only saw the injured Blue Jay one day. Unable to fly well - unable to use its feathers for full protection against the cold - it probably did not survive for long.

Sunday morning I saw a large dark circle atop the snow with a mound of red in the middle. When I went out to fill the feeders, I inspected. Beneath the three foot circle of downy feathers, the white snow was stained red. Bloody breast bones were picked clean. Part of the head remained to confirm the identification. The flock of thirty Mourning Doves which visit my feeders every morning had been reduced by one. A Cooper's Hawk, the likely predator, had fed well.

The amusing antics of the chickadees, titmice, and nuthatches are serious business; there is nothing "cute" about them. These birds are in a race for life - contending with winter storms, freezing temperatures, and dangerous predators. Most of us have solved the problems of food and warmth during the winter. We have the luxury of warm dwellings and stocked pantries. We lighten the long, dark nights with neighbors, singing nowell clearly. We cosy down with the miracle of light and carols of hope. But the danger and struggle is never far off. On the other side of the window pane, the birds are in a race for life.

Great Horned Owl

CHAPTER 30

WHAT I HAVE IN COMMON
WITH ROGER TORY PETERSON

Several years ago, I did a day of local birding with a couple of friends. After an early cup of coffee, we stepped outside to begin our count. Within minutes, we had twenty-five species, from several different swallows overhead, to feeder birds, to warblers singing in the trees. Stepping across to the beaver pond, an American Bittern posed on the edge of the grasses.

Then we began the harder work of finding the birds that were sitting quietly, or not singing but busy with nest building, or that had slipped past our first visual and auditory survey. I began scanning across the grassy field. Distantly there was a dark object in the field looking back at me. Although it was just about at the limit of my binoculars, two tufts on its round head were apparent.

Quietly I said to my two companions, "Great-horned Owl." I gave them a visual marker and they strained through their binoculars.

"Cat," said one.

"Is not," said I.

"No doubt. Cat," said the other. I continued to study it. Maybe, I thought.

"Time to find more birds," said one. "The one in the field only has feathers stuck in its teeth." We moved toward the car to begin our travels through the county.

Several times during our long day of birding, one or the other would say something like, "Maybe we'll get another Great-horned, or not." Or, "Hey, I got another cat."

We finished the day in the dark, listening to Barred Owls calling back and forth. Finally one said, "Guess we're not going to get another Great-horned." The other said, "And we've already got a few cats. Let's go home."

A couple of weeks ago, one of these companions telephoned in the early morning to warn me that a bear had taken his suet during the night. A day later he told me that he had seen the bear curled up in the grass near the distant beaver pond. "Are you sure it wasn't the neighbor's black retriever," I asked.

"You're trying to make my bear into your Great-horned. Won't work. It was a bear."

I was glad he reminded me about the cat that I called a Great-horned Owl. He does that about once a year. We got it over with early this year.

It was the kind of a gaff that lives on and on, alluded to subtly - or not so subtly - when the ego begins to crowd acceptable limits. Nevertheless, my enduring embarrassment gives me something in common with Roger Tory Peterson, the man whose field guides taught tens of thousands of people how to bird and whose name is as synonymous with birds as that of John James Audubon.

In 1937, Peterson's field guide (the first edition was published in

1934) had already given him a national stature. He joined long time friends of the Bronx County Bird Club for the Christmas Count. On a lake, his count group saw a Dovekie, a small pelagic bird that belongs in oceanic waters. Peterson studied it carefully. It did not dive, or even move very much. Drawing on his experience and reputation, Peterson told "my less experienced companions that its presence so far inland could be accounted for by the heavy wind and fog that had blown in from the oceans two days before. As an afterthought, I added that the bird looked rather sick and probably wouldn't live through the night."

The small group continued to study the apparently ill Dovekie. Several in the group thought they saw the bird move its head. Peterson agreed.

Some of the young men of the Bronx County Bird Club could be very raucous. When one of Peterson's companions on the count, Danny, puffed himself up and proudly announced the sighting of the Dovekie, these young men pounded the table ten times and shouted, "Horsefeathers."

When others came to Danny's defense, they pounded the table and shouted, "Horsefeathers." When Roger Tory Peterson finally weighed in, they pounded the table and shouted, "Horsefeathers."

Here's what led to the table pounding and horsefeathers. Danny was suspected of having a vivid imagination. When he was alone, he was able to see some rare bird that no one else saw. Someone carved and painted a decoy Dovekie and planted it in the lake. They were sure Danny would see it and insist that he had gotten the first Bronx record for a Dovekie. The announcement would be followed by the derisive roar and the revelation of the hoax.

What the pranksters could not have imagined was that the prank would draw in their target, Danny, others birding with him, including more than one who would attain wide recognition and stature among ornithologists and birders, and Peterson himself, whose reputation was already established.

Ten years later, Peterson related his embarrassing fallibility in his book *Birds Over America.* The incident never went away. A wooden decoy was seen to "move its neck" and was duly reported during the Christmas Count compilation party. Peterson, himself, confirmed the sighting. Fifty years later, the story was still being told back and forth by friends.

Said Peterson, "Well, at least we identified the species correctly."

I learned the story of the decoy Dovekie from *Birdwatcher, The Life of Roger Tory Peterson* by Elizabeth J. Rosenthal. For over fifty years, this skilled, self-taught bird watcher taught people how to watch birds with clear field guides and engaging prose. The biography fills out the life of the artist, photographer, writer, conservationist, editor, and traveler. And ... I learned from the biography that I have a shared birding experience with Roger Tory Peterson. When birdwatching, we both had an enduring, never-let-you-forget-it embarrassment.

Of course, Peterson had only the one experience of making a red-in-the-face misidentification. With me, the owl/cat was a major red-in-the-face misidentification. Unlike Peterson, I make smaller misidentifications all the time. But, I have a good time when I'm out birding anyway, and that's what is important.

Mute Swan

CHAPTER 31

SWAN SONG

Most birders are not fond of Mute Swans. They are non-native, and like many introduced species, they compete with native species. Some of that competition is a threat, or potential threat, to native species. In general, I share that lack of fondness for the Mute Swan. However, a recent visit to the Turners Falls area caused me to do some reconsidering.

There are several areas around Turners Falls, Massachusetts, where waterfowl and gulls gather, particularly in the Fall and Winter. It is an area where, for example, wintering Common Goldeneyes can usually be seen, along with the occasional rare Barrow's Goldeneye. Mixed in among the common gulls (Herring, Ring-billed, and Great Black-backed) there is the possible Iceland, Glaucous, Lesser Black-backed, and perhaps something even rarer.

On one occasion last month, the pickings were unusually slim - a few geese and Mallards, a single merganser, and the common gulls, though not as many as usual. Scattered along the canal and in the lake behind the dam were Mute Swans - about fifty. They are big white birds. Their orange bill is prominent. They do not pose any particular identification problem. They don't need much watching.

But there wasn't anything else to watch. After the obligatory grunt and dismissive bah, I watched the Mute Swans anyway. Eventually the castle wall of prejudice developed a few cracks; I found myself admiring the beauty, the sinuous curving lines, the ease and grace of these birds as they glided effortlessly through the water. I began to glimpse the swan for what it has been - an inspiration to poet, bard, painter - to those who weave tales of the unexplainable with images from the observable world around.

The Mute Swan is native to Europe and western Asia. It is non-migratory, one of the largest birds still capable of flight, monogamous (perhaps), aggressive in defense of its territory and young. Graceful. Pure white. Silent.

The common name comes from its silence. They can hiss and grunt, and do so when defending their territory, but unlike most waterfowl which announce their presence with barks, quacks, squeaks and rattles, the Mute Swan is almost eerily silent.

From this silence comes ancient folklore that the swan sings only once in its lifetime; the swan song is the single sweet song which the swan sings as it is dying. Socrates (in *Phaedo*) admonishes one of his friends who is protesting his imminent death: "And you seem to think I am inferior in prophetic power to the swans who sing at other times also, but when they feel that they are to die ...." Swan song is the last act, the final creative work, the farewell appearance.

The symbolism associated with many birds and animals is often quite consistent across many cultures. The lion is a symbol of power.

The dove a symbol of peace. The fox a symbol of cunning. Symbolism associated with the swan has little consistency. In some regions it was considered a feminine symbol associated with the moon. Its presence was a sign of intuition and gracefulness, considered feminine attributes. The goddesses Aphrodite and Artemis were sometimes accompanied by swans.

More often, the swan was a masculine symbol. Its pure white color connected it to the sun, almost always a masculine deity. The swan was linked in ancient Greece to Apollo, god of the Sun.

Perhaps the most familiar presence of the swan in ancient myth is that of Leda and the Swan. The ever randy Zeus spied the beautiful Leda, wife of the King of Sparta. His Olympian lust aroused, Zeus nevertheless exercised a degree of circumspection. Changing himself into a swan, he allowed himself to be pursued by an eagle. He sought protection from his pursuer by falling into Leda's arms. She apparently was a willing refuge, for she allowed him to stay in her arms through the night, even though her arms also included her husband. Her husband enjoyed her charms. Unknown to him, so did Zeus, still in his swan disguise. Helen, eventually of Troy fame, was the result of Zeus' uncontrolled libido.

It is sometimes said that Zeus raped Leda in the guise of a swan, and that is how many Renaissance artists titled their depiction of the event. But "rape" only referred to the illicit nature of Zeus' lust; most artists depict Leda as, at best, passive about the whole affair, and most show her as a willing participant. It is an event from the mythological past which allowed, and still allows, artists to push the limits of the erotic. The Mute Swan is the artist's model for Zeus in almost all the paintings and sculptures of Leda and the Swan.

A familiar story, charmingly retold by Hans Christian Anderson, is "The Ugly Duckling." A duckling is mistreated because he is ugly; real ducklings are cute. But the ugly duckling grows up to become a swan, a bird of surpassing grace and beauty. The fable illustrates the deceptive nature of first appearances and teaches that true beauty grows from within.

The Mute Swan appears in many roles in the mythology of the world. Here is just a sampling. In Celtic myth, a pair of swans steered the Sunboat across heaven. In Norse mythology, two swans drank from the sacred well in the home of the gods. The water was so pure and holy that all things that touched it turned white, including this original pair of swans and all others descended from them. In Germanic myth the Valkyries, the warrior goddesses, had the power to transform into swans. One accompanied her human lover in war, flying over the battlefield in her swan's plumage. In Celtic and Siberian culture, stories existed of swans taking off their plumage and turning into maidens. In Hinduism, the swan is a vehicle for many deities. Persons who have attained great spiritual capabilities are sometimes called "Great Swan" on account of their spiritual grace and ability to travel between various spiritual worlds. Hindu iconography typically shows the Mute Swan.

The swan, coming by way of this vast array of mythological tales, has continued to inspire artists. Tchaikovsky's ballet, "Swan Lake," is just one example; William Butler Yeats poem, "Leda and the Swan," is another. Jean Sibelius composed two works inspired by Finnish epic tales of swans in the underworld. The swan figures prominently in two operas by Richard Wagner, *Lohengrin* and *Parsifal*.

"The Bonny Swans," a 1994 song by Loreena McKennitt based on a seventeenth century ballad, tells a tale in which a young woman is drowned by her jealous older sister in an effort to gain the younger sister's beloved. The girl's body washes up near a mill, where the miller's daughter mistakes her corpse for that of a swan. A passing harper fashions a harp from the bones and hair of the dead girl/swan; the harp, powered by the girl's soul, plays a swan song before the entire court, telling of the sister's crime.

There are problems with the non-native Mute Swan in our area. But the Mute Swan has been an inspiration to the bards and poets and artists for millennia - a symbol connecting us with the unknown - from the erotic to the sublime, from the mysteries of life to the mysteries of death. When bird watching can make some of those connections, it is good birding.

Yellow-rumped Warbler - in eastern N.A., "myrtle," - in western N.A., "Audubon's"

CHAPTER 32

BIRD NAMES

B ird names are often curious. The rules of nomenclature say that once
a bird has been named, it keeps that name, even if the name has no
bearing on what is subsequently learned about the bird. That explains
why, for example, the robin has never been renamed the reb-breasted
thrush but remains the (American) robin, because it bears a similarity to
the (Eurasian) robin which has a red breast. Or why the American
Redstart does not have "warbler" in its name in some fashion, because
it bears a superficial resemblance to European redstarts, all of which are
in the thrush family.

A curious aspect about bird names is that many of the common
birds which we know in the East are descriptive names, while many of
the birds found in the West belong to someone; they are so and so's bird.

Consider our eastern warblers. In the East we find the Yellow,
Chestnut-sided, Black and White, Black-throated Green, Black-throated

Blue, Blue-winged, Cerulean, Bay-breasted, and others. If not descriptive of the bird, the name may suggest their diet or where they are found: Myrtle (now Yellow-rumped), Worm-eating, Magnolia, and Pine. By contrast, among the western warblers we find Virginia's, Lucy's, Townsend's, Grace's, MacGillivray's, and Audubon's (now lumped with the Myrtle as the Yellow-rumped).

The names of our eastern sparrows, all nondescript little brown birds, are descriptive. Chipping Sparrows chip, Song Sparrows sing, Field Sparrows are found in fields, Swamp Sparrows in swamps, White-throated Sparrows have white throats, and White-crowned Sparrows have white crowns. Go out West and you will find sparrows that also have descriptive names (Sage, or Rufous-crowned), but you will also find sparrows that "belong" to Botteri, Cassin, Brewer, Baird, Harris and Le Conte.

Not a single one of our local woodpeckers has a proper name in its name (Downy, Hairy, Red-bellied, Pileated, Norther Flicker, Yellow-bellied Sapsucker), but in the West you will find Lewis's and Nuttall's Woodpeckers and Williamson's Sapsucker.

The Ruby-throated Hummingbird is the only regularly occurring hummingbird in the East; other species occasionally show up, especially in the Fall, but they are usually juveniles and are notoriously difficult to identify as a different species, even for many experienced birders. In the West you can find many species of hummingbirds and most have names descriptive of their plumage, such as the Black-chinned Hummingbird and the Rufous Hummingbird. But among those western hummingbirds there is also Anna's, Costa's, and Allen's.

In the East, many common birds have a slue of folk names, a situation which often caused confusion until the American Ornithological Union began imposing some order. I pick just a few by way of example. The Northern Flicker has been known as High-hole;

Wake-up; Harrywicket, and Yellow Hammer. The Chipping Sparrow has been called Chip-bird and Hair-bird and is still referred to as Chippy. The Common Yellowthroat is still, and will continue to be, called the "Wichety-wichety," and no amount of officialdom is likely to change that.

So why does the West have so many birds named for forgotten people? It goes back to the history of Europeans in North America. The Spanish came to the Western Hemisphere for gold; the French came for furs. The English came to stay. It was the early 1800s before curious naturalists began describing the flora and fauna of North America in any serious or systematic way. Alexander Wilson (considered the father of American ornithology) and John James Audubon were self-taught artists and naturalists, often pursuing their interests in neglect of making a living. By the time they began their work, people of European descent, mostly English, had been living in the eastern states for two hundred years. They were clearing the forests, struggling with the native peoples they were displacing, contending with a far-away monarch, and creating a new form of government. In the course of making a living, they noticed the potato bird which ate the bugs in their garden (Rose-breasted Grosbeak). They scattered the rice-birds eating their rice with bird-shot (Bobolinks). They enjoyed partridge (Ruffed Grouse) and gobbler (Wild Turkey) on the dinner plate. And they listened to Stake-driver, Thunder-pumper, and Dunk-a-doo in the marshes (American Bittern). When the naturalists went to work describing the birds of the East, many of those birds were already very familiar. The naturalists provided some system and order.

At the beginning of the 1800s, President Jefferson pulled off the greatest land purchase in history, but had no idea what he had bought. The Lewis and Clark Expedition was the first of many organized excursions by the English-speaking Americans to discover what lay

140

westward. These expeditions were all sent out with instructions to record the plants, animals, birds, geography, and people to be found in these new lands. Accompanying the expeditions were naturalists (albeit often self-trained naturalists) charged with fulfilling these instructions. Hundreds of new species were recorded and collected, and eventually found their way back to the East. This continued as the frontier pushed its way to the Pacific coast and exploratory expeditions gave way to permanent settlers. Western species were new to everyone. With no folk names, the naturalists were free to do the naming.

Modern science was still in its developmental stage in the early nineteenth century, but already it was well-established that the person who discovered a new species - that is, described a new species for science - had the right to name it, and the name would continue thereafter. It was not appropriate to name a species after oneself, but you could honor someone by giving that person's name to a species you discovered. Audubon, for example, named a rare eastern warbler (non extinct) and sparrow after his South Carolina friend, Dr. John Bachman. Other Audubon friends and companions were honored in Harris' Sparrow and Harlan's Hawk (now a sub-species of the Red-tailed Hawk). It fell to others to honor the pioneers of American ornithology. Alexander Wilson fared quite well; his name is attached to a warbler, plover, snipe, and storm-petrel, and also to a genus of warbler. Audubon did not fare quite so well. An Atlantic shearwater is named for Audubon, and the western warbler which is now a sub-species of the Yellow-rumped Warbler. The western species called so and so's, were discovered and described by various naturalists and named by them, often honoring someone.

Eastern species which are named for a person are typically unusual or rare species; they were not well known to the general population and therefore could be discovered and named (Kirkland's Warbler, for example). In the East, birds bearing a place name, like Cape May, Tennessee, Connecticut or Nashville Warblers recall the place where they were first "discovered," not where they live. The four warblers just named winter in the tropics and breed near or north of the Canadian border. They merely pass through their place names during migration. On the other hand, western birds named for a place are likely to be residents of the place, like California Thrasher, California Quail, and Arizona Woodpecker (previously known as Strickland's Woodpecker).

I haven't begun to exhaust this topic of bird names, but it's time for a cup of coffee.

An uncommon Glaucous Gull

CHAPTER 33

GULLS AT THE TREATMENT PLANT

One January, I spent a long, cold morning at a waste water treatment plant in southeastern New Hampshire. I was not learning about the technological niceties which convert thousands of suburban flushes into potable water which can be safely returned to our rivers and lakes. That technology is important, but like almost everyone else, I don't give much daily thought or concern to how my environmental impact is cleaned up.

I was at the waste water treatment plant to look at birds - specifically, gulls. There were also lots of Mallards and Black Ducks. A raven cronked over head. Pigeons cooed. I did not see the resident wintering eagle which flies over the treatment plant once a day and sends the gulls fleeing for their lives.

Gulls were the attraction, and there were a couple thousand to look at. The normal three were abundant, or common. In the abundant category were Ring-billed Gulls and Herring Gulls. Ring-bills are North

America's most common and widespread gull. They are always close to water, but never far from shore. They do much of their feeding on land and can often be seen foraging or resting on grassy expanses, farm fields, docks, landfills and other habitats impacted by humans. The same can be said for the larger Herring Gull, though it is more likely to forage farther from shore. In the common category is the Great Black-backed Gull. Our largest North American gull, its size and dark black back make it conspicuous. It has been expanding its range southward along the Atlantic coast and along the St. Lawrence River and southern Great Lakes. Ring-billed, Herring, and Great Black-backed Gulls are virtual "gimmes" when birding during winter in the Northeast anywhere near any sizeable body of water.

These three gulls are omnivorous, and they are scavengers. They love landfills and garbage dumps. Not far from the treatment plant where I had hundreds of these gulls to watch, there was a large landfill. Hundreds more were swirling in the air above the landfill. After breakfasting on the tasty offerings of the landfill, the gulls flew off in various directions to rest until dinner time. One of those resting places was on and around the settling lagoons of the treatment plant.

Obviously, the dozen birders wandering around the lagoons were not there to see these common gulls. We were looking for the less common gulls which are almost always scattered among the huge flocks of common gulls. And specifically, we were looking for a very rare accidental - a Slaty-back Gull. This gull resides along the coastlines of northeastern Asia and winters south to Japan and Korea. In the summer, it regularly visits western Alaska. On very rare occasions, a Slaty-backed Gull fails to read its range map correctly and shows up at widely scattered locations in North America. Such is the case this year. An adult and a third winter bird have been seen and photographed at or near the water treatment plant in Rochester, NH.

I won't keep you in suspense. The Slaty-backed Gull did not visit the treatment plant the day I was there. After about three hours, my semi-birding companion complained about the cold and we left. Fortunately for her, the bird was not seen the rest of the day. But the Slaty-backed Gulls are still in the vicinity and are reported a couple of times a week.

However, the day was hardly a loss. Among the hundreds of common gulls there were several rare, but regular, gulls. The Glaucous Gull is a large, pale Arctic species. The ones that wander south are often sub-adults, first or second year birds, and almost completely white. A Herring-sized white gull is almost certainly a Glaucous Gull. Unlike the common gulls we usually see, it has no black wing tips. Whether at rest or in flight, its wing feathers are, at the tips, white or very pale gray. At the treatment plant, a white second year Glaucous Gull rested peacefully among hundreds of Herring and Ring-billed Gulls.

In one of the lagoons, the other rare but regular "pale" gull was busy feeding. A half dozen sub-adult Iceland Gulls were gleaning whatever tasty organic matter was swirling in the water. Also an Arctic species, the Iceland Gull is subject to extensive discussion about its taxonomic relationships. I will spare you the details, except to say that if you ever hear about a "Kumlien's Gull," the reference is to a subspecies of the Iceland Gull; the scientific classification is subject to much debate. Okay, just a little of the discussion: Kumlien's might be an Iceland, or a Thayer's, or a cross between Iceland and Thayer's, or its own species, or .... This is one of many questions which scientists haven't resolved, either because they haven't found the grant money to do the necessary study, or because a resolution would mean one less thing to argue about.

A third rare gull often mixed in with large flocks of the common gulls, is the Lesser Black-backed Gull. This is a European species which has become a more common visitor to North America in recent years, an increase which may be related to a growing breeding population in Iceland. Some think it may be breeding in Greenland or North America, but this has not yet been proven. The Lesser Black-backed Gull is closer in size to the Ring-billed Gull; its back is more slate-gray than black. Unlike most other gulls we are likely to see, its legs and feet are yellow, not pink. I have seen the Lesser Black-backed Gull on several occasions, but on this cold morning, I had my best opportunity to study it and compare its size, shape, and markings with many other gulls.

Waste water treatment plants, like landfills, are magnets for gulls who opportunistically feed on the organic by-products of modern society. Birding such places sometimes requires a tolerance to unpleasant odors. On this particular cold and windy day, the odors were either frozen or wind dispersed. I am not going to insult you by implying that I enjoy birding at treatment plants. I much prefer a hedgerow, an old logging road, or even the feeders in my backyard. But sometimes one just has to go where the birds are.

Good birding does not necessarily equate with magnificent landscapes or delicate floral bouquets. The day before I visited the treatment plant, I was in Boston at the Museum of Fine Arts. There I enjoyed the magnificent landscapes of the Hudson River artists, and could almost smell the flowers in a Dutch still life. So I had recent aesthetic fulfillment just before I visited the treatment plant. Sometimes good birding means that you have to hold your nose or just study the field marks of a gull, ignoring the fact that it is ripping apart a bag of rotting garbage.

And then, you have to have the ability to put those sensory experiences out of mind as you sit down to dinner.

Magnolia Warbler

CHAPTER 34

HOW TO SEE MORE BIRDS ON A BIRD WALK

Modern computers are remarkable for their ability to collect, sort, and analyze data. I have scarcely begun to tap the potential of the desk top version that I own. In spite of all of the electronic advances, I still rely primarily on the gray matter computer which I've owned for a lifetime. That computer lumbers along, occasionally connecting experiences into a conclusion that a more capable computer would have arrived at long ago. Consider, for example, this apparently random collection of experiences:

During the summer, I love to sit on the back porch sipping a cold tonic and watching the birds at the feeders. When the tonic gets low and I rise for a refill, the birds scatter. Once I settle quietly again, they return.

In late June, I hiked Oregon Mountain in Newfane. Somewhere off the trail, I heard a Magnolia Warbler sing. I stalked through the undergrowth. Near a small clearing in the forest with tangled brush and snags, I sat on a log to rest. After a couple of minutes, I saw the Magnolia Warbler, so I stayed put. In the following twenty minutes, birds appeared in every direction: Common Yellowthroat, Yellow-rumped Warbler, Winter Wren, Downy Woodpecker, Red-breasted Nuthatch, Black-throated Green Warbler, Black-throated Blue Warbler, Hermit Thrush, Red-eyed Vireo, Blue-headed Vireo, Ovenbird, Blackburnian Warbler, Blue Jay, Eastern Wood-Pewee. When the shadow of a hawk passed overhead, the birds disappeared. I made my way back to the trail. Before leaving the trail and finding the log on which to sit, I had heard a few bird songs here and there. After resuming my hike, I heard a few bird songs here and there, but nothing like that quiet time of sitting.

Someone once told me about going on a bird walk with David Sibley (of the Sibley guide.) The "walk" consisted on strolling a short distance to the brushy edge of a large meadow with a stream meandering through the grasses and willows. For half an hour they stood while Sibley identified songs and calls and verbally described where the birds were singing or calling from.

Juvenile birds flocked to my feeders this summer, drawn by the easily found food sources. Young Downy Woodpeckers especially liked the suet, and were reluctant to leave the tasty basket. As I walked across the lawn with a pan full of mixed seed, the youngster pecking away at the suet stayed put, pecking away. I felt like I could reach out and pick him off with my hand. Young Chipping Sparrows were equally clueless. I was practically opening the top of the feeder before they flew. So I assumed a surrogate parental role to those young birds. "Hey guys, there are dangers out here! You best learn a bit of wariness or you're going to be a Sharp-shin's dinner." And I clapped my hands with a "Hey! Hey!" until they flew. One young male Downy was a slow learner; he left the suet reluctantly. I didn't hold much hope for him.

Surveying for the Breeding Bird Atlas project in early July in Stratton, I heard a Swainson's Thrush singing. I followed the song into the thick spruce forest, stopped, and listened. The thrush was singing nearby, but I couldn't find it. It was close, so I stood still. Movement in a low branch was not the thrush; it was a Dark-eyed Junco feeding a fledgling. Another movement was a Black-throated Green Warbler feeding a fledgling. Yet another movement was a young Blackburnian Warbler calling for food; I watched as its father came quickly to feed its young offspring. I never did see the Swainson's Thrush, but while standing still among the thick spruce, I confirmed the breeding presence of three other species.

There are many similar experiences, plus anecdotes from other birders, which I have collected over the years - collected, but never connected. Until about a week ago when my gray-matter computer lumbered to the kind of conclusion which might prompt those modern cultural philosophers, the Simpsons, to respond, "Well! Doh!"

It's obvious. When I rise from my rocking chair and walk toward the bird feeders, the birds flee. I am invading their space. I am a potential danger - a threat - and they scatter. When I sit down again, they return, and feed ... until I move an arm. Then they scatter again.

Is it any different when I walk in the woods? I am an intruder - a gigantic intruder, fifteen times their size, and hundreds of times their bulk. Think of the monster-infested B movie ... how people flee before Godzilla. To an Ovenbird that may stand just over five inches in height, I am of Godzillan proportions. If he continues to sing as I approach him, it's because his hormonal need to control territory or attract a mate has overridden his better sense. And then I look at him with these mutant eyes of a truly alien creature. (Binoculars, in case your computer is working slowly today). Or I point something long at him (arm and finger) and somewhere in his genetic memory he recalls that long

149

straight things pointed at him once blasted fatal pellets in his direction. He doesn't know that I am voyeur, not a hunter or specimen collector.

But if I stay still long enough, then he no longer sees a threat, and will resume his courtship, his territorial defense, and his foraging ... as will his neighbors.

So my conclusion and/or theory is that a bird walk should be more sit, than walk, and might better be termed a "bird sit." A year ago I was walking the circumference of a field in Cape May. An elderly gentleman was sitting on a stool looking at the trees and shrubs lining the field. I greeted him. In return, he told me where the Yellow-billed Cuckoo was perched. I would have walked past it had I not met this man who was sitting. At the time, I thought his "bird sit" was a concession to his having several additional decades over me. Now I'm wondering if he may not have been exhibiting the quaint truth that wisdom comes with age.

I plan to test my conclusion/theory when I go on bird walks next Spring by doing more sitting than walking. In preparation for this field test, I have made an addition to my Christmas gift wish list (it's a very short list, because I have enough "stuff"). I would like a very light-weight, fold-up, three legged stool, with a carrying strap. I may even leave a dog-eared catalogue lying about, strategically open and highlighted in red. Of course, if the subtle hints of this column and that catalogue are not grasped by the appropriate gift giver, that will pose no impediment. I will simply outfit myself before the Spring "bird walk/bird sit" season arrives.

Test this theory for yourself. See if you don't see more birds when you sit than when you walk.

Bobolink

CHAPTER 35

BOBOLINK

The place where I stopped along the dirt road was quintessential Vermont. At the far end of the open meadow a red barn was surrounded with fencing. In the muddy barnyard two horses milled. In the adjoining pasture, three cows grazed. An old tractor idled near the road. Barn swallows swirled above the pasture and meadow, going and coming through the open barn doors.

Forest surrounded the acres of open field, but the forest did not block the vista from the hill crest where I had paused. Rolling hills stretched before me, verdant incarnations of the green mountains of Vermont.

A few days before I had contended with the endless strip malls and box store collections around Philadelphia and the Jersey shore. Now I breathed deeply the peace of a quieter time. Save for the distant chug of the tractor, the only sound was bird song - the rattle of a robin, the caw of a crow over head, a Savannah Sparrow singing in the field and a Song Sparrow in the brush behind me. And of course in the field the blackbirds sang - the creaks and scratches of the red-wings and the grackles as they rushed about in the Spring rituals of courtship, territory defense, nest building, and mating.

Blackbirds were the reason I stopped by this large, open grassy field. I wanted to see if they had successfully made the long flight from southern South America, returning to their summer home on this hillside field in Vermont. Like a good neighbor, I wanted to welcome them back, although I knew they would be so busy with domestic duties that they would not have a moment to spare for me.

So I leaned easily against the car and looked across the swaying grasses. Little black spots popped into the air, almost in the way bubbles rise in a champagne flute, but without the order. Accompanying the randomly swirling dark feathered bubbles was a complex, random string of musical bubbles. Two of the dark spots rose into the air, pouring forth so much song that they might have been mistaken for a whole flock of songbirds.

The Bobolinks had returned. One settled atop a shrub. The other chose a grassy stalk. Across the field a dozen others perched on a fence post, the shaft of last year's mullein, or whatever rose ever so slightly above the surrounding field. A rival came near, only to be chased off, or a female passed close, only to be chased after.

When the flying black silhouettes settled for a moment, they could be seen for what they are: confused blackbirds wearing their sleek black tuxedos wrong side front. Most birds with contrasting plumage are light underneath and dark on top. Not the Bobolinks. Decked out in their breeding finery, the males are entirely black on face, neck, chest, and belly. A buffy patch covers the back of the head and neck. The scapulars (those feathers which might be likened to the shoulder) are white; so is the rump. The effect is bold and striking - something like a groomsman wearing a white cummerbund with buffy ruffles on his shirt, except put on backwards.

Bobolinks are Icterids - blackbirds. In many respects, they are very un-blackbird like. They are small for blackbirds. The females look like large sparrows - buffy and streaked and generally nondescript. Unlike the most common blackbirds in our neighborhoods, they can also sing.

Boblinks are grassland birds. They are still relatively common breeders in southern Canada and northern United States. They like grass prairies, pastures and hayfields. Their numbers have declined steeply in recent years - as much as 50% in the last forty years by some estimates. In Vermont, the return of forests has reduced much of the Bobolink's former habitat, while the need of modern farming for multiple hay cuttings (as early as mid-June when young are still in the nest) has further reduced its habitat.

One folk name for the Bobolink is "skunk blackbird," a reference to its supposed color resemblance to the unpopular animal. In general, however, the Bobolink (the name is thought to represent its cheerful song) has been welcomed on its breeding ground; New Englanders often referred to it as the "meadow-wink." Early naturalists reported its appetite for insects, while farmers seldom reported damage to grain crops.

But in the southern states, the attitude toward the Bobolink has been very different. There the "rice birds" were killed, perhaps by the millions, in order to reduce the damage they caused in ripening rice fields in the fall and to the sprouting grain in the spring. They were also heavily hunted for food, appearing on restaurant menus as "reed birds," and considered a delicacy by gourmands, especially when the menu price was exorbitant.

This type of slaughter has been ended, and like all migratory species, the Bobolink is now protected. Habitat loss is a challenge for the Bobolink on its breeding grounds, but that does not explain the steep decline in recent years.

A few years ago, Dr. Rosalind Renfrew, conservation biologist with the Vermont Center for Ecostudies, began studying Bobolinks on their wintering grounds in Bolivia, South America. She discovered the largest single winter concentration of Bobolinks ever recorded; two adjacent roosts contained in excess of 130,000 Bobolinks. The area is a big rice growing area, and the "rice birds" are considered a pest by many of the farmers. But the real threat to the Bobolinks is from pesticides. Rice farmers apply large quantities of pesticides with a "more-is-better" approach. These agricultural chemicals are restricted or banned in the United States and are rated Class I toxins by the World Health Organization. From blood samples, Dr. Renfrew has documented severe physiological effects on Bobolinks from these toxic substances.

These colorful and musically adept blackbirds face toxic threats in their winter homes and loss of habitat in their summer homes. Twice a year they migrate thousands of miles through dangers which would daunt a dozen Indiana Joneses. In smaller numbers they occupy our grassy fields and meadows where they can find them.

Edward Forbush once described the Bobolink as a "happy-go-lucky fellow," and "a reckless, rollicking sort of a fowl, throwing care to the winds, and always bent on a lark," an effervescent bird expressing irrepressible joy.

As I watched them percolating above that grassy meadow, I knew the Bobolinks were really just doing their own Bobolink thing. But they filled me with effervescence and joy. And I wondered if we might have the good sense to make things a little more friendly for the Bobolink. A a friendlier world for the Bobolink will also be a friendlier world for all of us. I prefer that to a moment of good birding by a Vermont field.

Cooper's Hawk

CHAPTER 36

"GISS"

Field guides all have their limitations. For many species, there are so many variations in their plumage due to age, molt, sex, and season that a field guide can be an exercise in frustration if the user is looking for an exact match.

Early this week, I had a sparrow on my platform feeder which had a prominent white band on the back of its neck. Had I gone looking in a field guide for such a sparrow, I would have come up empty. Except for that white band, everything else about the sparrow was Chipping Sparrow, and the only puzzlement was why the white band. Perhaps it was nothing more than ruffled feathers, or an incomplete molt, or a quirk in the feathers' pigmentation.

The illustrations in older field guides were heavily dependent upon museum specimens. With a bird skin in the hand, an artist often saw details that are seldom seen in the field. Those details are not always seen when the bird is a living specimen flitting through the leaves as it feeds, or chasing a rival from its territory.

Modern field guides rely much more on field experience and field observations. Whether they are paintings (e.g. Sibley), digitally enhanced photographs (e.g. Kaufman), or a collection of many photographs in many settings and light (e.g. *Stokes Field Guide* or *The Shorebird Guide*), modern field guides are more likely to convey the visual "impression" of a bird than do the guides of a generation ago. Visual precision is not their purpose. In fact, there is a "Companion" to field guides that does not have a single illustration (Dunne). It does with words what field guides try to do with illustrations.

The exceptionally skilled birders who create these field guides and companions are attempting to incorporate their long experience of watching birds - namely, that identifying a bird in the field often relies upon recognizing the general impression, size, and shape of the bird in question. The shorthand for this identification technique is "GISS." Sometimes you may see it referred to as the "gizz" or "jizz" of a bird. British birders, in line with the quirky spelling of the Brits, are likely to use the latter terms.

Whether the acronym is rendered with an "s" or a "z," a "g" or a "j," it refers to the same thing - what is the impression or "feel" that a bird conveys. Don't let the idea of a bird's 'giss" scare you off. Most people already have some sense of "giss" when it comes to birds. If you see something fly to a tree and land upright on the trunk, clinging to the bark in an erect posture, you know that the bird is some kind of woodpecker, and you have already narrowed the identification possibilities from several hundred to a half dozen. If you see a silhouette creeping down a tree trunk, head first, you know that it is a nuthatch, and around here there are only two possibilities. In the spring and summer when the morning is just beginning to lighten, you see something running across the fresh cut lawn, pausing, cocking its head to one side, repeating, then pecking at the ground; you know that an American Robin is looking for worms. In each of these instances, you do not need long and detailed study. You have grasped the "giss" - the general impression , size, and shape.

The next step in using "giss" when watching birds is being observant. The Tufted Titmouse and the Black-capped Chickadee are closely related. Both like sunflower seeds. Both take one seed at a time to a nearby branch, hold it between their feet, and pound it open with their beak in order to get the meat inside. On a dark, gray winter day, you see a small bird on a branch in the back of the yard pounding on something between its feet. Chances are you can tell whether that bird is a titmouse or a chickadee, even before it comes back to the feeder for another seed. You have been watching both species for days, and the "giss" gives away their identities.

The main tool of the early ornithologists was the shotgun. They knew their birds because they held them in their hands. Today bird watchers have quality binoculars and scopes, digital cameras, field guides, bird song recordings, and a network of experts connected by e-mail, cell phones, and blackberries. But all of these tools and connections still can't help when the bird is distant, or on the move, or similar to a hundred other birds in a flock. That's where the accumulated observations and experiences of bird watchers has begun to collect and codify as the "giss."

"Giss" is especially useful when dealing with birds that look similar. In your field guide, thumb through the section on seabirds or shorebirds. Even in the quiet of your armchair and with no distracting television, grasping the differences between the species within these groups can be daunting. For many avid bird watchers, that is the attraction of these birds. By observation, they learn the behavior and sense the impression, and thereby make identifications.

Casual visitors to Putney Mountain may see a dark speck in the sky and listen as the hawk watchers quickly say, "Sharp-shinned," and scan elsewhere for the next speck. They may suspect that the hawk watchers are practicing their own equivalent of voodoo economics. In fact, the "giss" of a Sharp-shinned Hawk makes it one of the "easy" hawks to identify in flight: a snappy wing beat - flap, flap, flap, glide - all wing and no head and a long skinny tail - an "attitude" that doesn't hesitate to attack another sharpie, or any other bigger bird in the vicinity.

But then there are those times when a bird doesn't "feel" like a sharpie; the wing beat is more deliberative, or it appears to have a lot of head. The "giss" says Cooper's Hawk.

A field guide might tell you that a Golden Eagle has a "golden" head and neck, but that field mark is useless when the bird is flying high overhead. An impression of an eagle with a smaller head, of plank like wings which somehow do not move quite the way a Bald Eagle moves its wings, of wing set that may look like an Osprey, or at other times like a Turkey Vulture - all are part of the "giss" that says, "Golden."

General impression, size, and shape is a method of identifying birds used by the backyard bird watcher, and the obsessive bird chaser. It is not mysteriously esoteric. The differences are merely in degree. "Giss" means that we have gotten a little more connected to our natural world. Instead of the natural world being apart from us, it becomes a part of us. We begin to know what we see, even though we may not know how we know.

Carolina Wren

CHAPTER 37

CONTINUING WITH "GISS"

Let's continue with the "giss" of bird watching - recognizing birds by their general impression, size, and shape. Often our sighting of a bird is very brief, in bad light, partly obscured by leaves, far off, or in a myriad of ways anything but adequate in making a field guide identification. But general impression, size, and shape may point in a direction, or even allow a definite identification. I had two very different experiences with "giss" in recent days.

A week ago, I made a trip to Dead Creek Wildlife Management Area in Addison to see the Snow Geese, and perhaps locate a Ross' Goose. Often the geese feed in the hayfields and cornfields near the goose viewing area. Not this time. During the several hours I spent around the goose viewing area, they never came close. They spent a lot of time flying around - north, then south, back and forth. A couple of thousand geese flying high and low in the sky overhead is an impressive sight. But when they landed, it was on a pond behind a distant rise.

Why the geese were behaving the way they did was a mystery. I hoped the Fish & Wildlife manager who stopped to talk might have an explanation, but he was even more mystified.

While talking with him, I kept alert for other birds, especially hawks. Over a nearby field, I saw the long, vee-shaped wings of a bird flying low over the grass, dipping and rising and dipping again, hovering, and then dropping into the grass - a Northen Harrier. I watched this harrier off and on for most of the morning. It was a male, gray above, white below with black wing tips and trailing black on the wings - a gray ghost.

The most distinguishing field mark for the harrier is its large white rump. This marshmallow, as many bird watchers refer to it, is often visible even when the bird is at a great distance. However, the harrier's style of hunting over grasslands and marsh conveys impression, size, and shape which is distinctive and makes it identifiable even if the marshmallow is not seen - in fading afternoon light or when it is just a shape over a far-off field.

The Northern Harrier is a hawk with owl characteristics. Like the owl, it has a round facial disk of feathers which act like a parabolic dish to gather in sound. But its facial disk is much smaller than that of an owl, so it hunts with a combination of sight and sound, dipping and rising as it looks and listens for its prey. The "giss" of this hunting style makes it possible to identity the harrier even at a distance. In addition to the nearby male harrier, I saw three more harriers hunting over distant fields, identifying them by their "giss.".

A few days ago, I received an e-mail from a reader in Wilmington who reported a hawk over her mowing field. I am very hesitant to offer an identification based on someone's verbal or written description, but this person provided an excellent account of the bird's "giss": about noon, "this beautiful whitebird flew down from the trees way up the hill surrounding the mowing and headed straight forward, glided between two apple trees (only about 100 feet from my house) then turned flapped up and flew horizontally down almost to the level of the grass and seemed to pause and hang there as he must have been looking for something to eat. He quickly flew up again and did this several times before leaving heading west."

She described the hunting style of a harrier, and her impression of a white bird further identified it as a male harrier (the female is a brown bird, streaked underneath). A final note: around 11 am on the same day, hawk watchers on Putney Mountain saw a male harrier flying from the northeast to the southwest, in the direction of Wilmington, sixteen miles away. Very likely the same bird was seen at both places.

Now I go from a large, magnificent bird whose "giss" is very helpful when identifying it, to a very small bird which showed up in my backyard late yesterday afternoon.

Going through the kitchen, I did a quick look at the sunflower feeder. I saw the back and tail of a small bird disappear behind the feeder. I did not see the head, beak, or breast. All I saw was rich brown on the back and tail, and a tail which seemed long and thin. It did not give the impression of any of the regulars which come to my feeders. The color and shape and tail was not right for any sparrow or finch.

Something in the impression triggered "wren" - perhaps a sense of an up-cocked tail. House Wrens summer in backyards and should have gone south by now. Marsh Wrens lives in marshes and should have gone south. Winter Wrens lives in the woods and should have gone south. That leaves the Carolina Wren, which has extended its range northward, sometimes lives in towns and villages if it can find the undergrowth it likes, and does not migrate.

I had grabbed a "giss" - a general impression, size, and shape that said Carolina Wren. I saw a lot of Carolina Wrens when I was birding in Florida and Cape May this Spring. Occasionally I lingered over them, because they have that irrepressible wren energy and enthusiastic wren song that makes wrens so much fun to watch. But I did not always linger; they are common in those parts, and I was looking for the less common. However, I've never seen a Carolina Wren in my backyard. Having gotten the "giss" of a Carolina Wren on my feeder, I sat down, and waited and watched.

After a few minutes, my "giss" was confirmed. A Carolina Wren crawled around the sunflower feeder, ate seeds that had fallen in the tray, and posed very nicely for me - with his bright white eye strip, his butterscotch colored breast, his chestnut brown back, and his speckled, up-tilted wren tail. He was, by the way, the ninety-sixth bird I have seen in, or from, my backyard.

Merlin

CHAPTER 38

SURVIVAL

A woman walking through the Putney Meadows in mid-November a few years ago found a small bird fluttering on the ground and unable to fly. It was a Horned Lark. She called me to ask what could she do. I referred her to a neighbor who is a licensed wildlife rehabilitator.

When I spoke with my neighbor a few days later, I asked what had happened. He told me that the bird had no apparent injuries, but it was weak and emaciated and within a couple of hours, it died.

Most readers have probably found a sick or injured bird at some time, and perhaps you have tried to restore it to health. The probability of success is low. Even an experienced wildlife nurse fails far more often than he/she succeeds, and the smaller the bird, the greater the incidence of failure.

Our desire to rescue injured or sick birds is commendable. It demonstrates a compassion for the weak and a regard for the sanctity of life. A creature which has received the gift of life should be entitled to enjoy and retain that gift. When something happens to threaten the gift of life, we feel compelled to intervene and remove the threat. I am as susceptible to this attitude as anyone else.

And so it is hard to admit that in holding this attitude, I am giving in to a romantic and simplistic view of the natural world - a world in which the issues of life and survival are far more complex than I care to acknowledge most of the time.

Let me continue with the emaciated Horned Lark. Horned Larks gather into flocks during the winter. They frequent open fields, walking and running on the ground as they search for seeds. They are relatively abundant in our area as long as the ground is still free of snow. How then did one Horned Lark come to be alone and on the edge of starvation? Perhaps when a falcon made its appearance, it flew right, while the rest of its flock flew left, and it became disoriented. Perhaps it was the runt of the nest, weakest from the moment of hatching. Through the concerted efforts of its parents, it was able to get enough food to grow and fledge, but it always struggled to catch up to its stronger siblings. Perhaps it just never learned how to uncover hidden seeds, finding only the most open and obvious food. Whatever the reason, it did not possess the fitness required for its individual survival. And in the scheme of nature, the survival of any species demands a fitness far beyond that of mere individual survival.

But that does not mean that the weak Horned Lark served no purpose. Like all small birds (and some large ones), it is a vital part of the food chain.

Let me shift focus from our barren November cornfields to a southern seacoast where a hatch year Merlin spends most of his day perched on a scrubby tree. Twice a day, morning and evening, this small falcon needs to eat. His food source is the wintering flocks of small sandpipers. With long, pointed wings, this fast flying predator captures his prey in midair.

In the early winter, the young Merlin takes young, weak sandpipers - the ones which barely had the resources to make their long migration. Later he takes the ones whose reflexes are slower, or who lack experience to take instantaneous flight with the rest of the flock - the ones who delay a fatal half second. As the winter progresses, the young Merlin's hunting skills improve, as they must - for he has culled out the weak, the sick, and the inexperienced. He must now have the strength, reflexes, and instinctive hunting skills which are a shade keener than the concomitant survival skills of the sandpipers which so far have escaped his attacks.

By the end of the winter, two things may have happened. A young male Merlin will have the hunting skills to provide for himself, the mate he will find, and the young which he will help raise and to whom he will have contributed his genes. Second, the sandpipers with the best eyesight, alertness, foraging skills, and reflexes will be the ones who will make the demanding journey to their breeding grounds - the final test to determine who is best suited to continue its species' gene pool.

For both predator and prey, it is a difficult and demanding task. Only a few of the Merlins fledged in any year will survive long enough to breed. Among shorebirds, researchers have seen evidence that a third to a half of wintering flocks are taken by falcons. What happens with falcons and shorebirds is happening with all other predators and prey as well.

Back to our barren fields. During the third week of December, Audubon volunteers do their annual Christmas bird count. On that day, I can imagine wandering through some old wind-swept orchard. From the distant grasses, a flock of Snow Buntings takes to the wing. Their numbers are noted. Someone in our small group suggests that a larkspur was among the flock, but no one else can confirm it. In a gnarled apple tree, something moves slowly from branch to branch as we come closer, but it doesn't fly. I'm close enough to see that it's an Eastern Bluebird, even without raising my binoculars. Still it sits there, and I wonder if I could walk over and pick it out of the tree . Another of our group diverts attention from the fluttering bluebird to a hatch year Sharp-shinned Hawk perched on the low branch of an oak tree at the orchard's edge. It is alert, sharp-eyed, and poised. We redirect our steps to other parts of the orchard, and areas closer to the protection of the car.

We might wonder why the sharpie and the bluebird have not gone further south as most of their kind have done, but we leave them both to whatever awaits each. Perhaps the sharpie will attack, and feed, insuring its survival ... for the moment. Perhaps the bluebird will flee to the thicket and continue its life ... for the moment. Perhaps ... perhaps - there are many "perhaps." We move quickly away from the slow moving bluebird and the perched hawk, leaving both undisturbed by our presence. As the frigid wind bites through the layers of clothing, we are for these moments free of romantic notions of an Eden-like natural world. Our task on this winter day is to observe and count, not to intervene.

Partial webbing between the toes of this young Semipalmated Plover accounts for its name, "semipalmated."

CHAPTER 39

SHOTGUN ORNITHOLOGY

Ornithology means the study of birds. Like the other sciences, today it is a profession entered by means of a Ph.D. from a university. A person who studies birds, but does not have the credentials, will have "ornithologist" tempered with the adjective, "amateur." Or more likely, ornithologist will be avoided entirely; terms which do not imply an academic background will be used instead, such as naturalist, and perhaps birder or bird watcher.

It was not always so. Alexander Wilson, often called the father of American ornithology, was born in Scotland to a family of weavers and sometime smugglers. As a young man, he wrote libelous poetry, was convicted of blackmail, and at twenty-eight, penniless. He came to America. In Philadelphia, he found a library to explore and gradually hit on the idea of writing a book about all the birds of America, a book which would include his own illustrations. He taught himself to paint.

John James Audubon's ornithological training was similar. The illegitimate son of a Frenchman and his maid, Audubon had the good fortune to be acknowledged by his father and receive some education. Like Wilson, Audubon taught himself to paint, though he would sometimes claim to have studied painting in France.

Although both Wilson and Audubon were self-taught, their paintings were the basis of their reputations. However, that was not the most important skill to their ornithological pursuits. The most important skill for these pioneers, a necessary skill which continued into the early twentieth century, was the ability to use a shotgun.

There may have been some primitive optics floating around, but nothing that could be used to study the birds. Mist netting, bird banding, and DNA studies all lay far in the future, as did illustrated bird guides. The only way to learn anything about the physiology of a bird, to compare that physiology to the physiology of other birds and thus establish relationships between species, was to have a specimen in hand. And that meant blasting it out of the tree, pond, marsh, or air with a shotgun. In his *Birds of America,* Audubon often writes of the beauty and grace of a particular bird, of being transported to a state of bliss by a bird's song, or spellbound by courtship behaviors. He then adds, matter-of-factly, that after observing these behaviors carefully, he "collected" a specimen.

"Shotgun Ornithology" - that's the term which Scott Weidensaul uses in his new history of birding in America, *Of a Feather.* The leading ornithologist in the late nineteenth century firmly believed, Weidensaul writes, that "the path to ornithological wisdom issued from the muzzle of a shotgun." This ornithologist recommended that the beginner collect all the skins he (almost no "she's" at this time) could: "Say fifty or a hundred of any ... species" (!! - exclamations added). Ornithology was a bloody science, and it yielded its blood lust very slowly. The professionals sneered at the opera-glass ladies who dared suggest that there might be another way.

Technology has revolutionized the study of birds, but the legacy of that shotgun science continues. Today there are still vast collections of bird skins in museums, universities, and research facilities, and every bird watcher is the beneficiary of those collections. The modern field guide on which we depend in order to make our identifications could not have come into being without those collections. When young Roger Tory Peterson produced the first edition of his revolutionary field guide during the 1930s depression years, it was these collections to which he turned. David Sibley crisscrossed the continent to produce his *Guide to Birds*, published in 2000. He saw most of the 810 birds he illustrated, but not all. A few, like the Island Scrub-jay, which he did not see until 2004, required museum skins and photographs.

The length of a bird, wingspan, and weight are all routinely measured by bird banders. Audubon tied a string around a phoebe's leg to see if it returned to his Mill Grove home in Pennsylvania the next Spring (it did), but data collection by bird banders did not begin in a significant way until the early twentieth century. Prior to bird banding, specimens provided this data.

The superior field guides on which all modern birders depend are the most important legacy of shotgun ornithology for the average bird watcher, even if we don't recognize it. Another legacy are some bird names. Many bird names are descriptive; they make perfect sense and are even helpful. You see a warbler with a black throat and blue back and you know you are seeing a Black-throated Blue Warbler. You see a hawk with a red tail and you know you are seeing a Red-tailed Hawk. You see a woodpecker with a bright red head and you know you are seeing a Red-headed Woodpecker.

But then there are the birds who owe their common name to the aftermath of a shotgun blast when they could be studied in the hand.

Along the seashore and river sandbars, it is easy to identify the small Semipalmated Plover, but the similarly named Semipalmated Sandpiper requires careful observation to distinguish it from other small sandpipers. The name provides no help. "Semipalmated" is from the Latin "semi" meaning "half" and "palma" meaning "palm of the hand;" it refers to the partially webbed foot of the plover and sandpiper. When staring through binoculars or a scope, you will be lucky to see anything of the foot of either bird as they forage on mud flats, floating seaweed, or in shallow water. The name was given by a shotgun ornithologist.

Are you looking for a prominent ring on the neck of the Ring-necked Duck? Don't. The "ring" is a faint line of lighter color at the base of the neck, a feature barely distinguishable in the field guides, much less in the field.

How about the Sharp-shinned Hawk? This is another characteristic you should not look for through your field glasses, even if it is a perching bird you are looking at. The "shin" refers to the lower leg of this bird below its ankle (the tarsus). The tarsus of most land birds is rounded. On this bird there is a raised ridge on the front of the tarsus. The "shin" is "sharp" - hence "Sharp-shinned."

Most of our swallows are named for where they nest: tree, barn, bank, cliff, cave. But then there is the Northern Rough-winged Swallow. The "rough-wing," according to *American Bird Names*, refers to "the recurved hooklet on the outer web of the first primary feather"!! *Pete Dunne's Essential Companion* transforms the name of the Northern Rough-winged Swallow's into something helpful when he suggests that its plumage "seems somewhat disheveled or shabby - rough!"

One final word about shotgun ornithology. Although many collections contain drawer after drawer of bird specimens, the number of birds killed for science over the years is nothing compared to the carnage produced in a single night by a skyscraper or TV tower, or the annual toll from domestic and feral cats. Enough birds have been sacrificed in providing you with a good field guide with which to identify birds. Don't add to the number. Keep your cat indoors!

Mallard

CHAPTER 40

OPEN WATER

When I make a trip from South Newfane into Brattleboro, I have a list of things to do, places to go, errands to run: recycling, bank, library, hardware, grocery. Often I factor in time for coffee, lunch, or browsing. Commonly I plan time for stops along the river, or the Retreat meadows, or parks or trails to check on the bird life. I call this research for my writing.

From December through the first week in January, my yellow pad list for a trip to Brattleboro factors in an extra hour for ice skating on the meadows. This is one of the most delightful activities of the entire year and I grab at every opportunity - gliding about that expansive pond ... stopping to look through the glassine ice at objects beneath the surface ... greeting neighbors ... watching one of several pick-up hockey games ... smiling as a young child on skates for the first time teeters along, while the family dog gambols encouragingly by her side.

I don't do any active bird watching when I am skating on the meadows. Maybe I should. Maybe I should carry my binoculars with me to check the gray bird atop the cherry tree and be sure it is a mockingbird and not a shrike. But my purpose is to enjoy the ambience of place and people, to feel the biting cold on my cheeks, the burn in my legs as muscles are called on for unfamiliar exertions.

Oh, I am aware of goldfinches twittering overhead. I may pause to watch the gulls scavenge some remains tossed by an ice fisherman, or left by an ice picnicker. I may look up once in a while at the crows passing by, or notice a Red-tailed Hawk trying to climb on a weak winter thermal.

Once on the December meadows, I saw a Cooper's Hawk perched atop a pigeon. Beneath the still pigeon, red stained the smooth ice. The Cooper's looked around in every direction, as though worried. It appeared uneasy, and flew off, leaving its meal on the ice surface. I followed its flight to a tree along Route 30, then felt movement on the periphery and turned back to see a Red-tailed Hawk land on the ice next to pigeon. He looked about, hopped on the prone pigeon, surveyed the meadow and sky overhead, then flew off with the pigeon in his talons.

But any of this bird watching is happenstance during that week or two when the Retreat meadows are frozen and the community gathers for its spontaneous ice skating party. As the time approaches, I carry my skates in an old mud bucket in the back of the truck, prepared to alter plans when the figures on the ice tell me it is time for skating.

During this period in December and early January, there is only one acceptable reason why I might not linger for an hour of ice skating. The reason is that the ice has become covered with several inches of snow. Then I may have to re-plan my whole day so that I "happen" upon some suitable spot for snowshoeing or cross country skiing.

That is how I plan my errands in town during this season of the year. And when the skating is really good, I don't even need an errand to justify a trip to town. The good ice is reason enough.

You understand then, that I was not happy early this week when I made my yellow-pad-in-hand trip to Brattleboro. The sunny day felt like late March. The Retreat Meadows looked like ice-out, except that ice-in hasn't even happened this year. I wasn't wearing my winter wool coat - just a sweat shirt. No gloves. No hat. No ice skates.

I grumbled. If I want a New Jersey winter, or a North Carolina winter, I can move there. But I like New England winter. I like the cold and the snow. I like watching the chickadees through my kitchen window while inches of snow accumulate. I like it when I have those rare encounters during these months with neighbors, pale from the winter darkness and cranky about contending with the elements, but wonderfully resilient and resourceful.

I would like to blame someone for the open waters in the Retreat meadows so far this year, but I don't know who. There are so many possibilities. I guess I'm just cranky, not from winter, but from the lack of winter. I tell myself that I need to take a page from those old Vermonters about being resilient, resourceful, and adaptable. And so, as I approached the open waters of the Retreat meadows earlier this week, I wondered if the absent winter might have caused some ducks to hang around. Just south of the I-91 bridge, I checked the West River and saw birds on the water.

I slowed, then stopped. The guardrail obstructed my view, but it seemed as though ducks were diving. Wonderful, I thought. Maybe they're Ring-necked, or possibly scaup. I couldn't see profiles very well, but Ruddy Duck might be possible, or goldeneye. I grabbed my binoculars and car dodged across Route 30.

Yes, there were several dozen ducks, and some were diving. I took a closer look at the smaller and nearer group. Mallards! - dabbling ducks

- puddle ducks, as a friend calls them. But what about the diving ducks? I counted five Mallards. Then there were six Mallards, then seven. An eighth popped to the surface. They mingled together, then two dove, and another, and another, until there were only three on the surface. I looked at the larger group further out. There were twenty plus birds, and they were diving as well. All Mallards. They were diving with the same alacrity as the most adept diving duck.

Diving ducks, such as the mergansers or goldeneyes, have feet which are relatively nearer to their tail. This helps them to dive and swim underwater. Dabbling ducks, such as the Mallard, Northern Pintail, or teals, have feet which are relatively more central to their body. They feed by upending themselves, with tails pointing up and neck stretched down to forage on vegetation. Their feet can often be seen waggling in the air.

But I was watching dabbling Mallards dive. It happens - not often, but occasionally. I have seen it before in the winter. Sometimes a bird guide or resource will even mention it.

I watched the Mallards in the West River for a while. The males are beautiful birds, often ignored or overlooked because they are so common. I enjoyed the opportunity to focus on the Mallards as they engaged in their unusual diving activity. Yes, I enjoyed watching them ... though not as much as I would have enjoyed gliding across frozen ice. We have to make the best of what is given us.

Common Raven

CHAPTER 41

COMMON RAVEN

S tanding on the ridge of Putney Mountain and looking west over the
West River Valley, I could almost imagine being one of the early
European settlers to arrive in the county. I could see a patch of cleared
land along unseen Newfane Hill Road, and another set of green fields
along unseen Wiswall Hill Road, but the rest appeared from the top of
the ridge to be unbroken forest canopy. Of course, this flight of fancy
meant not letting my eye take in the ski slopes which slash down the
sides of Mt. Stratton or Mt. Snow, or the wind generators at Searsburg,
but that's what flights of fancy are - selective in their assessment of
reality. But my flight of fancy did not have to filter out the "cronk,
cronk" which carried distantly on the crisp air. Not since the forest was
cleared for farms and sheep pastures has the "cronk, cr-r-r-uk," the
"crank, kraaaak" been heard over these ridges and hills as it can be heard
today.

Jock, the native Vermonter standing next to me, had helped me locate those surviving hill farms. "Kraaak, kraaak." He made a half turn and pointed. "There he is." Propelled on the brisk updraft, a large black bird popped above the ridge, flapped and glided, banked and turned, tucked wings and disappeared below the ridge as quickly as it had appeared. "Cronk, kraaak." "Crank, cr-r-r-uk." Two of the black birds popped above the ridge, then a third and a fourth. Individually - or in tandem - they tumbled and swirled, soared and tipped and dove, mastering the wind, defying gravity and looking for all the world like they were having a lark.

And perhaps they were. It's only been a few years, a few generations, since the ancestors of these enthusiastic juveniles reclaimed their place in these hills. So they may have been celebrating their return. But more likely, they were just having fun.

The Common Raven. Oh! - the commonality and dearth of imagination from the committee that named it. The raven may be big and black, but it plays the air currents with such alacrity, that one can hardly call it "common." A magnificent flier, it can hold motionless in a gale, hover like a kestrel, soar like a hawk, dive like a peregrine, fly wing tip to wing tip with its one true love, and tumble over and over in the air.

The raven is a passerine - a perching bird, a "songbird." At twenty-five inches perched, it is the largest songbird, larger than most hawks and about a third larger than its cousin, the common American Crow. It is best known by its wedge-shaped tail in flight, its thick bill and its shaggy throat feathers ... and its voice: "cronnnkkk," deep and echoing, mixed up with screams and gurgles.

I saw my first raven in 1982. A scenic rest area just west of Wolf Creek Pass in southern Colorado provided a stunning view of the valley between mountain ranges. Atop a rocky pinnacle, a raven surveyed his remote wilderness home. The raven maintained his place in the mountain and boreal forests, on the cold tundra and the dry deserts. This shy and wary bird watched the European settlers cut the eastern forests and blast their guns at anything that walked or flew. It retreated. By 1900 (and probably much earlier) it was virtually gone from the East. When Edward Forbush wrote his *Natural History of American Birds* in the 1920s, he had so little experience with, or personal knowledge of, the raven, that he had to quote extensively from another ornithologist.

I recorded my second raven in 1992 on Cadillac Mountain in Acadia National Park. A pair soared along the slopes of that rugged coastal dome. Except for rare nesting pairs in the high elevations of the Appalachian Mountains, the northern Maine coast was still about as far south as the raven was likely to be seen.

Then during the 1990s, ravens became much more common in the forests of eastern North America. Scientists are unsure whether this is a result of more forest cover and the maturing of eastern forests, or a behavioral shift by the ravens toward greater tolerance of humans. Tolerance of humans may be a risky behavioral change, but the two of us watching the youngsters frolicking on the brisk winds were glad they had taken the risk. Perhaps they were the ones Jock saw being fed in the field behind his Dummerston farmhouse in the middle of May.

About twenty years ago, Bernd Heinrich, University of Vermont biologist, studied winter ravens at his cabin in the remote forests of Maine. His research established that raven pairs (they pair and mate for life) stay on their territory through the winter, while younger birds gather in far-ranging nomadic groups. The groups of juveniles and unpaired younger birds cooperate in the foraging of food and use the social interactions of the group to establish pair bonds. Hence, on Putney Mountain when a group of four or more ravens are playing on the wind, I surmise - reasonably, but not certainly - that they are young birds whose parents have sent them off to make it on their own. These youngsters find one another and together learn, share, and hone their survival skills. They also have a grand old time showing off their flying skills.

Heinrich concludes his *Ravens in Winter* with these words: "An unmated raven finding food invites eligible singles to join him (or her?) at the feasts, thereby not only gaining or maintaining access to the food, but possibly also increasing its status and demonstrating fitness as a future provider for rearing offspring. It is an elegant, simple, and beautiful system. But it is clothed by intricate detail and subtlety. As far as I know, no other animal shows a similar system."

"Croook-croook." "Cur-ruk Cur-ruk." The wildly variable conversation of the uncommonly Common Raven. I get an internal flutter whenever I hear those raven "songs."

Rock Pigeon

CHAPTER 42

TOUGH CITY BIRDS

During the last snow storm of the season (I hope it was the last!), a pair of starlings came by the suet feeder. Since the beginning of the month, their large winter flocks have been breaking up in anticipation of the breeding season. Just before the snow storm, they had been singing and courting in the trees around my home, and today I saw them emerging from the barn attached to the house. Starlings are cavity nesters, and one of their favorite cavities in my neighborhood is the empty space in a wall of my house.

The pigeon flock that lines my roof ridge has not dispersed, but there is a lot of pigeon flirting going on among the crowd as pairs seem to be forming and reforming.

But why mention these birds? European Starlings and Rock Pigeons, along with the smaller House Sparrows, are birds which birders love to hate. All three are abundant exotics. They are not native to North

America. They compete with native species for nest sites and resources. The starlings, for example, pair early and nest early, often using cavities which might otherwise be used by woodpeckers, small owls, or kestrels. House Sparrows, also cavity nesters, compete with bluebirds and swallows for nest sites. They are often nuisances and hazards. Starling flocks clog jet engines. Pigeon poop erodes buildings. None of these are loveable birds.

But they are highly successful species, and they have honed their success in the one of most severe habitats imaginable - the city.

Nearly every city and town hosts large flocks of pigeons. We see them swirling over the Brattleboro skyline and roosting along the roof ridges. Historically they nested on rock ledges, bushes, and squat trees. Now they use bridge abutments, bell towers, and building lofts. In Brattleboro, I recently watched pigeons coming and going in several stone retaining walls. Like starlings they are early nesters. By mid-May they will have fledged their first brood and will be nesting again. For 5000 years, pigeons have lived in towns and cities, adapting their life style to the human made environment. When they have filled the niche, they have taken their adaptive survival skills into the surrounding countryside. And so they crowd the bird feeders at my rural village home.

What is it about these city survivors that makes them so successful, and prolific? The subject came to my attention by a brief article in *Sierra* (March/April 2008) titled, "Sex and the City Bird." The article began: "City folks have always seen themselves as a breed apart, tough survivors. Turns out that urban birds, too, may be of a heartier strain. In probing this premise, we at *Sierra* found ourselves asking some unexpected questions: Is citified sluttiness a survival trait? Does busting a hip-hop move help a metrosexual bird thrive where his country cousin might fail?"

Science is just beginning to probe questions related to the coping mechanisms of urban birds, but some of the early research is suggestive. There is, for example, some evidence that urban birds are more likely to flirt with strangers. In European cities, Great Tits (a smaller version of our chickadees), have dropped low-frequency notes from their songs in favor of higher-pitched, fewer, and stronger notes than their country cousins; this is in response to the noise of urban traffic. Male European blackbirds in the cities develop gonads sooner, begin mating earlier in the season, and have longer reproductive cycles than those living in the rural areas.

In North America, there are a number of native species that have learned to cope with the city and town. My daughter lives in an old mill section of Philadelphia. Spring and summer, I am always surprised at the variety of birds I hear singing or calling in the early morning; in addition to the hated three, I typically hear the cardinal, robin, mockingbird, yellowthroat, dove, House Wren, Downy Woodpecker, and Song Sparrow.

Our American Robin (closely related to the European blackbird which is also a thrush) is one of the most adaptable species, thriving not only in the city, suburbs, and towns, but in forests, farms, and even as far north as the Arctic tundra.

Walking the streets around my daughter's home, I was surprised one day to hear the clear, mimic sounds of the mockingbird. These birds have been called "urban winners," often thriving in cities and towns. Some of their success may be attributed, in part, to their nests being less vulnerable to predators such as snakes.

A few years ago, my son-in-law was looking out of his office window in a downtown skyscraper in Philadelphia. On a building roof below him, he saw a pigeon. The pigeon was providing dinner to a Peregrine Falcon. Peregrine Falcons naturally nest on bare cliff ledges.

They were brought back from the brink of extinction and, in addition to returning to historic nesting sites, they began pioneering places with new "mountains" and unclaimed "cliff ledges" - on bridges and high-rise buildings. One of the first of these Peregrine Falcon urban pioneers established its nest on the Verrazano Bridge between Brooklyn and Staten Island.

Urban dwelling Peregrine Falcons have given researchers easy access for studying their nesting practices. New Hampshire Audubon has monitored a pair nesting in a Manchester building; by banding the chicks they have been able to study the dispersal and survival of the young falcons. In San Francisco, a Peregrine couple have become internet stars as they have "taken to cavorting for a 'nest cam' set in a wooden box filled with gravel on the 33rd floor of a downtown building. Their exhibitionism has earned them a worldwide audience ...." (*Sierra*)

It makes sense that Peregrine Falcons would take up residence in an urban environment. With abundant flocks of pigeons and starlings, they can hunt as their ancestors have hunted for millennia, taking prey on the wing at the end of a deep, fast dive; in the city, there is never a lack of prey. In fact, urban falcons and hawks (like Pale Male and Lola, the New York Central Park Red-tailed Hawks) are probably the most effective means of controlling pigeon populations.

Even so, there has yet to be any real research on how these urban raptors cope: Are there differences, for example, in their physiology, breeding practices, or migratory patterns from their wilderness counterparts? We don't know.

Nor do we know much about how or why the hated three in North America manage to cope. Coping mechanisms of the Rock Pigeon might be explained simply by the fact that they have been domesticated for 5,000 years, going feral for just as long, and living in, with, and among humans for that entire period.

But what about the House Sparrow which thrives in North America but whose population is declining in much of Europe? Or the European Starling which has also exhibited significant population declines in some parts of Europe?

Birders (professional ornithologists and amateur bird watchers) may not have much affection for the starling, pigeon, or House Sparrow. But these birds probably have something to teach us if we ask the questions, look for the answers, and can overcome our prejudices.

"Chewink," once known as Rufous-sided Towhee, is now Eastern Towhee

CHAPTER 43

WHAT NAME

A friend called to report that he had found a female Long-tailed Duck among Common Goldeneyes and Common Mergansers about two hundred meters below the Vernon Dam.

The report was interesting because this is heavy-bodied duck normally winters in small groups on shallow, open ocean. In its winter plumage, I expect to see the Long-tailed Duck whenever I make a winter excursion to the seacoast, especially in the harbors and estuaries. One spring I saw one in the West River. It baffled me at first, since that was the first time I had seen this duck in breeding plumage.

But my subject is about the name, "Long-tailed Duck," rather than the duck itself. Had my friend called me a few years ago to report a Long-tailed Duck, I am not sure I would have known what he was talking about - not because the duck in question was unfamiliar, but because a familiar duck had been given a new name. The name I have always known this duck by is "Oldsquaw."

The change was decreed by the American Ornithological Union (AOU). Founded in 1883, this is a professional association of ornithologists, and interested amateurs willing to pay the annual membership fee. The AOU is the organization which, among its other research and scientific pursuits, determines the taxonomy of birds in North America. It was the AOU which finally made the determination that the sub-species of the Gray-cheeked Thrush which nests in the spruce forest on the mountain tops of Vermont should be considered a separate species. The Bicknell's Thrush was "split" from the Gray-cheeked Thrush by the AOU.

The AOU determines how birds should be classified, and assigns or approves their scientific names (the Latin derived words that most of us can barely wrap our tongues around) and the common names by which most people know the species.

For the most part, we are fortunate to have one organization which makes such decisions. In Europe, there is no comparable authority, with the result that the same bird sometimes is classified and named differently from one place to another. Scientists and academics (in all fields, not just ornithology) are often stubborn, contentious and opinionated. When this impacts on taxonomy, the result can be confusion. In North America, the respectability and authority of the AOU means that we avoid most of the chaos. Publishers of field guides and check lists have a common standard with which to work.

That's not to suggest that the decisions of the AOU do not meet with criticism. For many years the discussion of scientists as to what constitutes a species resulted in the "lumping" of many birds. Avid life listers were especially upset by this practice, since every time two birds were lumped into one, it meant that their life list grew smaller. The prevailing theory was that if two birds (usually an "eastern" one and a "western" one) had overlapping ranges and were known to interbreed, then they must be one species, not two. This resulted in the "disappearance" of many long and often beloved species. To give just a few examples: The Baltimore Oriole and Bullock's Oriole became the Northern Oriole. The Red-shafted and Yellow-shafted Flickers became the Northern Flicker. The Rufous-sided Towhee and the Western Towhee became the Rufous-sided Towhee. The Myrtle Warbler and Audubon's Warbler became the Yellow-rumped Warbler. Four different juncos became the Dark-eyed Junco.

Then came DNA testing, and the entire situation changed. There was now an independent, more or less quantifiable, means of determining whether forms of the same species were races, color morphs, or separate species. The result is that species which were "lumped" are now being "split," and that "races" of one species should actually be considered separate species. Among the examples given above, the towhees and orioles are again separate species, while the flickers and juncos are being reconsidered.

All of this I find interesting - sometimes even intriguing. With one exception. And that is: when the AOU determines a common name, they usually (but not consistently) try to be descriptive. In doing so, they seem to lack all sense of poetry. For example, when the Solitary Vireo was "split" into three species, our eastern form became the Blue-headed Vireo. Phooey! And moreover, it takes a lot of imagination even to see a blue head on our Solitary Vireo. (I will admit that "Blue-headed Vireo" is an older name for this bird.) When the towhee was split, the "Rufous-sided" vanished, to be replaced by the "Eastern" and "Spotted." Why not call it the "Chewink?" - which many birders repeat whenever they hear its familiar call, and is every bit as descriptive - of voice, if not appearance.

And then there's the Long-tailed Duck. As far as I know, this species has never been lumped or split, but its common name was changed. It used to be called "Oldsquaw" - a name probably deriving from the fact that this is our most loquacious duck, and when a group of them start crying together they sound like a pack of hounds (according to Forbush), or even a bunch of old squaws. However, that's not politically correct, so out it goes. But why not one of the other folk names? (Not "old wife" - that would get me in trouble at home.) "Scolder" is an old folk name, and my offspring might assure me that it could apply to either gender. Or how about "Scoldenore?" That has a ring of folk poetry to it.

In his account of the duck in question, Forbush includes this: "After a winter storm on our coast while the bellowing surf still beats madly on the rocks, one may see the vigorous Old-squaws riding on the face of a towering wave and diving in time to avoid the white and toppling crest - perfectly at home on the wintry sea. This is a species full of life and vigor." Wouldn't it be nice if the AOU could give it a name which captures that kind of vitality? - instead of Long-tailed Duck. So boring.

Ah well! I hope you see one, whatever you call it.

Dark-eyed Junco

CHAPTER 44

WINTER TO SPRING

Several weeks ago, a friend shared her opinion of Blue Jays. I don't remember her exact words, but they included noisy, nasty, and messy. I did my best to defend one of my favorite backyard birds, citing their beauty and intelligence. Their raucous calls alert other birds to the presence of predators. The seed that they scatter from the feeder to the ground benefits the ground feeders. "I know," she retorted, "they're messy!" I don't think I changed her mind.

With the calendar turning to March, I previewed the month ahead by reading *The Old Farmer's Almanac*. The "Farmer's Calendar" for March described the fierce competition around the bird feeders for seed, competition which takes place in spite of the obviously abundant provisions which are available. The column is written by a Newfane neighbor; he is seeing the same winter birds at his feeders that I am seeing at my feeders - chickadees, titmice, nuthatches, goldfinches, jays.

He wonders why the "war zone," the "aggression" and "chaotic free-for-all."

He muses: "Being weak, they ought to hang together, to share, to look out for one another. But no, they choose to squabble and fight instead. So we see in our winter visitors great charm, beauty, and peerless aerodynamics - united with a certain lack of moral intelligence."

So what is it that motivates a bird in its behavior, be it a nasty Blue Jay or an aggressive chickadee? At its very simplest, it is survival. In the summer months, it is survival of the species - the successful transmission of genes to the next generation. In the winter months, it is survival of the individual.

I am writing on the coldest morning of this winter. Feathers provide remarkable insulation against the cold, but unless the bird has eaten enough high-energy food during the day before, unless it has built up enough fat reserves to generate heat through the bitter night, it will not survive. I wonder how many birds did not make it through the sub-zero night? I have no way of knowing, but I have observed that the dove flock and the jay flock has been diminishing in number through the winter months.

When daylight returns, the birds must feed. They need to quickly replenish the fat reserves which they burned through the night. The first task of each individual bird is to survive as an individual, and that urgent task trumps every other motivation. Predators and breeding territories and finding mates are all irrelevant if I don't get enough to eat. There may be abundant food in the bird feeder, but just in case - get away from there! That's mine!

In yesterday's new-fallen snow, I went snow-shoeing on Black Mountain. From branches high over head, I heard an occasional "chick-a-dee-dee-dee." In the winter woods, resident song birds gather in loose flocks to forage. The flocks may include chickadees, nuthatches, woodpeckers, titmice, kinglets and even an occasional creeper. Most of the time they are relatively quiet. Their calls keep the flock together, and tell others where there is food.

The flocks also serve to gather many watchful eyes and to provide safety in numbers. A dozen or twenty pairs of eyes are more likely to spot the perched Sharp-shinned Hawk than are a single pair of eyes. When one in the flock spies a predator, it raises the alarm. Soon those quiet winter woods echo with warning calls.

Should that hungry hawk decide to attack, the odds of surviving that attack are much better if a bird is one among twenty, than if it is one among two, or one among one.

On this cold morning, the birds around my feeders were quiet. The jays were calling to one another from time to time (they can hardly go anywhere or do anything without talking about it), but mostly they were just eating ... and eating ... and eating.

In spite of the late February arctic blast, something different is beginning to happen. The Winter solstice is long past, the Spring equinox only a few weeks away. The days are longer. Free-for-alls about the feeders are more common, but I don't think they have to do with food. I think they have to do with sex. Winter is waning and the strong individuals, the alert and agile and elusive-of-predator individuals have almost made it through the winter. They have survived. Hormones are beginning to flow, perhaps stimulated by the longer light of day.

I see chickadees in twos and threes and fours dashing through the pine trees. They are not fleeing a danger; they aren't rushing off to another food source. I am seeing prologue to the spring drama, when defining a breeding territory, claiming a mate, and chasing off rivals plays over and over in our northern woods. By mid-April, many chickadees will begin their first nesting. The prologue will soon give way to the acts and scenes.

191

The titmice are at it. In the sparkling, clear air, they are whistling their love song: "peer, peer, peer." The titmouse song is the overture to the spring symphony. Wolf-whistles from the starlings rasp from tree tops. Soon we'll hear woodpeckers drumming, their species' way of saying, "This tree is mine."

A few species push the season even harder. Great Horned Owls are, or soon will be, on their nest. Our local eagles in Vernon have been repairing and expanding their aerie. If they follow their pattern of past years, they will begin incubating during the second week in March.

In spite of long underwear, lined jeans, and multiple layers of clothing, winter is beginning to give way to spring. This is transition time for the birds - transition from their sole concern to survive as an individual, to their need to extend the life of their species.

Nene

CHAPTER 45

THE SAGA OF THE NENE

M y trip to the Hawaiian Islands provided a few occasions to do some birding, and many occasions, then and since, to wonder about the travels and survival of birds. These islands are the most remote pieces of land on the planet. The nearest continental mass is 2000 miles away. How and why would land based birds ever find their way to these specks?

Pelagic birds were no surprise. Albatrosses, shearwaters, petrels, terns, boobies , and tropicbirds are legendary travelers adapted to living from the oceans. But the gulls, whom we associate with the oceans - mis-calling them seagulls - are absent from the Hawaiian Islands except for an occasional stray bird. Gulls don't like to be too far from land and seldom venture very far into the open ocean.

How then, for example, does a bird like a goose - one that makes its living from shallow ponds and vegetated fields - find its way across

2000-3000 miles of open ocean? It might be able to rest on the journey, but probably not feed. Why does it do it in the first place? Having done so, why doesn't it learn from its mistake, return to the continent, and never go astray again?

I discussed these questions in general with a scientist and that discussion stimulated what follows. But please don't blame the scientist - what follows may be more the product of my imagination than science.

Let's go back many millennia to a proto-Canada Goose, ancestor to our Canada Goose and Cackling Goose, of the Genus, *Branta*. It bred in the cold northern regions of North America and wintered in the warm regions, migrating between the two regions along continental shores and river valleys.

One year, something happened to a particular breeding group of this proto-Canada Goose that rewired the internal compass. Maybe it was a solar burst, or some local anomaly in the magnetic field. The result was that when these geese flew south, their course was 24 degrees to the west of their usual course. Unfortunately, that course of travel had nothing but open ocean until they reach Antarctica. They were never heard from again.

On another occasion, something happened to another breeding group that also rewired their internal compass. But this time, the result was that they flew south on a course that was 25 degrees to the west of their usual course. This course of travel took them to a group of islands spread across a couple hundred miles of oceans. They landed. They wintered. They bulked up, and in the spring, they returned to their breeding ground in northern North America. There, they bequeathed their rewired compass to the next generation, and they all returned to the islands to winter.

But one year when they returned to their breeding grounds, they faced a disaster. The summer was unusually cold; the grasses did not grow. The ponds and puddles stayed frozen longer in the Spring and froze early in the Fall. Food was short. The birds were unable to build up the fat reserves necessary for their long flight. But they were internally wired to fly south on a certain course. Lacking the energy reserves, they never made it to the islands, and they were never heard from again.

Back on the islands, a few of these proto-Canada Geese had not migrated remained for the summer. They were probably first year birds that had not yet paired and weren't ready to breed. They summered on the tropical islands, waiting for their kins-geese to return. But the geese did not return.

Now the story moves to firmer ground. Some proto-Canada Geese that remained on the islands began to breed and to evolve. They adapted to the scarcity of wetlands by learning to forage in lava fields and the semi-barren slopes of volcanoes. With a life-style that had less need to swim and more need to walk over difficult ground, they lost part of the webbing on their feet. Those proto-Canada Geese are still Genus *Branta,* but they are now their own species, known in the Hawaiian Islands as Nene (nay-nay).

It was a tropical paradise for the Nene. Unlike their continental relatives, they did not have to contend with Gyrfalcons, Snowy Owls, foxes, or any other predators. The living was easy and the dangers few.

The first predators to reach the Hawaiian Islands were humans; Polynesian colonists arrived about 1500 years ago. They also brought rats and dogs. The tame and unafraid Nene became food for the first time. But they survived, probably because they lived in an area between two great and mysterious volcanoes, Mauna Loa and Mauna Kea, an area which was forbidden and feared by the Hawaiians.

When the Europeans arrived, the situation changed dramatically and dangerously for the Nene and many other native species. Especially dangerous was the legacy of the New England missionaries. Their sons remained in the islands; they transformed the biblical injunction to "subdue the earth" into "exploit the islands," and continued the Puritan work ethic that had long since been transformed into "profit above all."

Needing something to sweeten their dour Calvinism, these missionary sons created pineapple and sugar cane plantations. But rats began eating into the profits, so they imported mongooses from India to control the rats. The mongooses found it easier to prey on the naive Nene. Having somehow survived in the distant past a perilous journey across thousands of miles of open ocean to find a home in a predator-less paradise, the Nene, descendants of those colonizing geese, were now in peril.

It gets worse. Those of European descent have developed the most efficient instruments for killing. And then, they have used those efficient instruments for sport hunting. By 1951, heavy hunting, combined with mongoose and feral cat predation, had nearly driven the Nene, still naive toward predators, to extinction.

Enter the Boy Scouts. With the help of the Scouts, Nene were rounded up and a captive breeding program was begun. For fifty years, captive bred birds have been reintroduced into the wild. On the island of Kauai, where there are no mongooses, these still naive Nene are doing well.

On Kauai, I finally saw several Nene in taro fields and again around the lighthouse in a wildlife refuge. The latter were tame birds, completely unconcerned by the human presence, tolerant even of the people stooping down to get a closer look at their nest beneath dense shrubs. The ones in the taro fields behaved more like a Canada Goose relative should behave. They were among drained fields and on the grassy dikes between the flooded fields. When I took tentative steps toward them, they watched me warily and stretched their necks. They objected to my presence: "Haw ... hawah." The posturing and vocal objections looked and sounded just like those of the Canada Geese on Sunset Pond when I come too close to their young in my kayak.

The Nene is Hawaii's state bird. It is endearing, still tame, and jealously protected by people trying to preserve their natural heritage. People with that kind of an attitude are one of the many things for which I am thankful.

Sharp-shinned Hawk (hatch year)

CHAPTER 46

IN SUMMER'S HEAT

This summer's heat, humidity and frequent rains have sent gardens into a wild and profligate production. Last week when the rains took a day off, I headed to the vegetable field in the early morning, intent on reaping the bounty and reestablishing control over the uncontrolled beds. I pulled and clipped and weeded and weed-wacked. I picked and pruned, sampling along the way. When the hour came when neighbors should have been well past the point of stirring, I began running the machines which make labor easier, even though they overwhelm the sounds of the world around.

By mid-morning I had reestablished some order among the chaos caused by life's exuberant display. The paths among the vegetable beds were cut; the most blatant of the weeds were pulled. Save for the pumpkin patch where the long runners continued to expand visibly in random directions even as I worked, the garden again looked tended. I returned to the house and barn, ready to give attention to the lawn and flowers beds.

There was a brief pause for coffee. Then, before heading into the shed beneath the barn for the next tool, I stood on the rise and looked over the Rock River which borders the back of my small homestead.

The piercing scream of a Blue Jay took my attention to the pine grove on the far bank. Screams followed in succession as a jay briefly dove from mid branches into lower branches. The blue flash was pursued by flashing brown and white wings.

I hurried to the river bank, hoping for a better, or another, glimpse. From behind the protective screen of willows, calling continued, and among the pine branches brown wings stretched, something in the manner that I have seen when a hawk is holding on. For that is what I had glimpsed in those brief flashes: a hawk in pursuit of prey. And since I never saw the jay emerge from the bushes or pines, I knew the hawk had made a capture.

I continued to watch, hoping that the hawk might fly from its cover and allow me to identify it. I wished I had my binoculars to penetrate the foliage, but I dared not return to the house, less I miss what little could be seen of the struggle across the river.

With only limited visual and auditory glimpses of what I witnessed, I am left to filling in the details with speculation, though it is speculation which I trust is reasonable, and which fits the evidence. Please read "possibly" or "probably" as I tell you what happened.

There were no other Blue Jays around at the time of the attack, and none to protest the attack or to attack the attacker, so the unfortunate jay was a juvenile, separated from its nest mates and parents, barely aware of dangers, inattentive and slow to react - fatally slow. A Sharp-shinned Hawk (or perhaps its larger cousin, a Cooper's Hawk) took advantage of the jay's youth. Superbly adapted to hunting in forest and thicket, the sharpie's short rounded wings and long tail allow it to maneuver through tree trunks and branches in pursuit of songbirds. The hawk ambushed the young jay, and in quick pursuit grabbed the panicked bird.

The Sharp-shinned Hawk was itself a young bird, not long out of the nest and on its own. It captured the jay in its talons, but the jay continued to call, to protest its plight, to plead its fate. The young sharpie was as inexperienced as a predator as the young jay was inexperienced in avoiding the predator. The young Sharp-shinned had made a capture, a critical success in its struggle to become a breeding adult. But it had not killed. It held food in its talons, but its prey continued to struggle, to call forlornly for help; the hawk stretched its wings to hold its balance against the throes of the jay. The hawk knew enough not to relax its grip; its survival depended upon the jay. Over long minutes, the call of the jay became weaker and then ceased. The young Sharp-shinned was a successful hunter; it was not yet an efficient killer, but that would come. One step at a time, and the first step is to learn through experience how to capture food often enough to keep up its strength for the next hunt.

There is another possible scenario that may be less grim to our human sensibilities. In this scene, the pursuing hawk was an adult Sharp-shinned, an experienced hunter and efficient killer. It took the young Blue Jay and quickly ended the struggle. A fledgling hawk followed its parent into the pine branches. In this scene the calling which I heard was not that of a captured Blue Jay, but of a young hawk demanding food from its parent. The wing movement which I glimpsed was the wing fluttering so common to birds which are begging food from a parent. The calling which became weaker, or softer, and less frequent, was that of a young hawk whose demands were being met and whose craw was being filled - of a bird which could not eat and talk at the same time. In this scene the Blue Jay meets the same fate, but with more dispatch. And soon the young hawk will have to hunt on its own.

I could see little of what was taking place across the river, and eventually I went back to my task of caring for the lawn and garden. Whatever the precise events may have been, my mind continued to replay them. It is a difficult and dangerous time for young birds. As I returned to my task of reordering nature's summer chaos, I found several places around the yard where there were little clumps of feathers, downy reminders of how difficult and dangerous summer's rush to life can be for some of that life.

By mid-afternoon my work was done. I was hot and sweaty and dirty. I stripped to my cutoffs. I was too tired to go inside to change and neighbors were too near to strip completely. I sat in the middle of the river. The heat and grime were rinsed clean.

Later, as I hung the heavy, wet shorts on the line to dry, my bare feet stirred a blue feather in the grass. Perhaps an adult jay had molted the feather. Perhaps a young jay had moved too slowly. The feather was ragged and broken ... and long ... a tailfeather.

Ruddy Turnstone flies 125 miles on 1 gram of fat

CHAPTER 47

ARISTOTLE

... On the Hibernation of Birds

Aristotle lived 2,400 years ago, in the fourth century before the common area. He was a Greek philosopher in the literal meaning - a lover of wisdom. Among his many interests was the natural world. As a naturalist, he observed and reasoned. Science in his day did not consist of experimentation or testing of theories. There was no messy lab work, and very little arduous field work. Why bother when the mind itself could arrive at conclusions through its own powers?

Among Aristotle's vast output was his ten volume "History of Animals." In this work, he refers to about 140 species of birds; some of his references to birds were on the mark. He knew the migration pattern of some large birds, such as Eurasian cranes. He described how other birds migrate from higher altitudes to lower altitudes. He observed that birds setting out on migration were fatter, and that those returning from migration were thinner. Today it is a given that migrants bulk up before departure and that they burn those fat reserves during their long flights, but it took 2,300 years before scientists elaborated much on Aristotle's observation.

Aristotle's travels were limited to the "civilized" world, which was restricted in the Greek mind to what is today Greece and Western Turkey. He might have watched cranes, for example, flying over head. Then he gathered reports from travelers who saw cranes in the marshes of the Nile River during winter, and from other travelers who saw them on the steppes north of the Black Sea during the summer. From this he was able to conclude that cranes migrated.

Unfortunately for Aristotle, it is not some of his astute observations and conclusions that are best remembered among naturalists today, but his mistakes. For example, in Greece there are five species of swallows, small, fast flying, insect eating birds. (One of them is the same Barn Swallow that nests in our barns, garages, and porches.) Aristotle knew that these birds disappeared during the winter, but he had no reports of them being anywhere else in the known world. In addition, I would imagine that it was inconceivable for him that such small birds could make a long journey. So with very thin evidence, he concluded that the swallows hibernate in the winter - hidden in holes, crevices, or hollow trees.

Try not to laugh. His conclusion was accepted wisdom for over two thousand years. In the mid-1500s, for example, the Archbishop of Uppsala in Sweden strayed from theology to natural science and declared the hibernation of swallows as "fact." When science began to enter the experimental stage, some researchers tried to induce hibernation in swallows by locking them in icehouses; the results were fatal.

Our American bird watching hero, John James Audubon, did a great deal to revolutionize the understanding of bird migration. He knew that many birds moved seasonally long distances. But old "facts" die hard. In 1878, Elliot Coues, one of the founders of the American Ornithologists' Union, was convinced that the insect-eating swallows followed food sources south; he knew they migrated. But he could not ignore the possibility of hibernation. He listed "182 publications dating back to 1630 that accept the possibility of swallow hibernation." He admitted that hibernation was "well attested, according to ordinary rules of evidence." He told his readers to weigh the evidence and make up their own minds.

Try to imagine Aristotle standing in Capistrano when the swallows return. Two millennia ago travel was slow and difficult. There was no way to track bird movement; the few ships that successfully returned from the "ends of the earth" were just glad to have survived. The rare person on board who might have been a curious observer is unlikely to have noticed tiny swallows flying about, and connect those swallows to the ones nesting in the stables at home in the summer. So when the swallows suddenly appear at Capistrano, is it so odd to conclude that they have emerged from hibernation?

Let's put Aristotle on Harvard Square in Cambridge, Massachusetts. He has concluded, logically and rationally in his mind, that some birds hibernate. It is quite easy in September to observe a small warbler in the Cambridge neighborhood (and all along today's New England coast) that is feeding voraciously. If we are observant, and it is quite likely that Aristotle was keenly observant, we will recognize that this small warbler is a Blackpoll Warbler in its rather dull, nondescript winter plumage. One day the bird disappears. Gone. With his students listening raptly, Aristotle tells them that the tiny warbler has gone into hibernation.

No, no, no, you say. This tiny Blackpoll Warbler has departed on its migration. Weighing about a half ounce, for the next four days it will fly 1800 miles nonstop over the Atlantic Ocean until it reaches the coast of South America, and then it will continue to southern Brazil and Bolivia. And Aristotle will tell you that if you are going to propose an alternate to hibernation, at least it should be reasonable and believable! His students are less restrained; they are rolling on the Harvard Square grass - or wondering where they can get whatever it is that you have been smoking.

After the breeding season, the swallows in Greece migrate to Africa or southern Asia. Aristotle had no way of learning this. He knew of animals that hibernate, and came to the reasonable conclusion that the swallows also hibernate. Writer after modern nature writer will recount this "ridiculous" conclusion on Aristotle's part with barely concealed derision, as though the "true facts" were not even more outrageous and beyond belief.

Bird migration is fascinating and astounding. It is no surprise that Aristotle could not conceive it for his swallows and postulated, instead, hibernation. He was wrong about the swallows. But - I hope you are ready for this - he was not wrong about hibernation.

***

... Some birds do hibernate.

Aristotle explained the winter disappearance of some species in a couple of ways.

One theory he proposed was "transmutation," whereby one species changes into a different species. For example, Aristotle said that the Common Redstart "transmutes" into the similarly sized and shaped European Robin (not related to the American Robin). The summer nesting Garden Warbler becomes the winter Blackcap. There is enough similarity between the last two species that his conclusion, on the surface, is not too farfetched.

The five species of swallow (including the Barn Swallow) with which Aristotle was familiar leave their breeding grounds in Greece to winter in Africa or southern Asia. Aristotle had no way of knowing this. Such long distance flight by small birds is almost unimaginable. Therefore, to explain the disappearance of swallows, Aristotle proposed "hibernation." As winter approaches, the small birds disappear into crevices, holes, and hollows, where they spend the cold months. They reappear with the warm weather, suddenly and in numbers. They have awakened from months of hibernation.

We have only learned about the remarkable migratory journeys of birds in the last hundred years or so. Many of these journeys are hard to believe. The Blackpoll Warbler, mentioned above, makes its nonstop flight over the Atlantic Ocean from the Maritimes and New England to South America in about 90 hours. Ornithologists studying this warbler suggest that the flight "is equivalent to a human marathon runner competing in 50 consecutive 26-mile (42km) races without consuming any food or water en route and without losing speed from the first to the last leg ... if this tiny bird were burning gasoline instead of body fat, it could boast a fuel consumption rating of about 720,000 miles per gallon." (Prius, eat your heart out.)

A female Whimbrel (a medium sized shorebird with a long curved bill) was fitted with a satellite transmitter in May, 2009. By mid-August she had been tracked from Virginia to Alaska to the Hudson Bay, more than 8,000 miles. On August 10 she left the Hudson Bay. On August 14 she landed on St. Croix, Virgin Islands, having traveled 3,500 miles in 100 hours. That's an average speed of 35 miles per hour.

The Bar-tailed Godwit breeds in Alaska. It winters in New Zealand. A female with a satellite transmitter "left Alaska on August 30 and arrived in New Zealand eight days later after a nonstop oceanic crossing measuring 7,250 miles ...." That's an average speed of about 38 miles per hour, over open ocean with no resting places. She slept on the wing.

With our modern scientific sophistication, we might laugh at Aristotle's notion that birds hibernate. However, the reality of bird migration is harder for the human mind to grasp than the notion of hibernation. If we did not have hard scientific evidence, we would dismiss each of these extraordinary flights as beyond all reasonable possibility. We can't walk five miles on the Appalachian Trail without consuming handfuls of high energy gorp, but a four ounce shorebird, the Ruddy Turnstone, can fly 125 miles and only burn one gram of fat. For that matter, typing at my desk is so strenuous, I just went downstairs to get a piece of left-over Halloween chocolate in order to keep my energy level up.

If any reader laughs at the notion that birds hibernate, you have little concept of what is reasonable, sensible, logical, and believable. It is far easier to believe, as Aristotle proposed and as all intelligent people for two millennia agreed, that some birds hibernate during the winter. Easier to believe that, than some of the incredible flights and migrations that some birds actually make.

At least, it is easier to believe Aristotle until we are confronted with the empirical scientific evidence. And let's not laugh at Aristotle. I am quite sure that were he reincarnated today, he would acknowledge his error in the face of the facts ... which cannot be said of everyone, judging by some of the crazy notions that are accepted today as fact (and my mind is made up).

I return briefly to Aristotle's other alternative to considering the migration of small birds: transmutation. When I compare an American Goldfinch in breeding plumage with an American Goldfinch in winter plumage, I see a pure bright yellow bird with a few stunning black highlights and a dull, nondescript, olive-drab bird. They are so different that a novice could easily think them two different birds. I don't know if there are any European species that undergo a similar dramatic change in plumage, but I can understand how Aristotle might postulate transmutation.

Aristotle was wrong about the five species of swallows that he knew in his Greek homeland. They do not hibernate. They migrate to Africa and south Asia after the breeding season is over. However, there are birds that do hibernate.

First a definition: "Hibernation is a state of inactivity and metabolic depression in animals, characterized by lower body temperature, slower breathing, and lower metabolic rate. Hibernating animals conserve energy, especially during winter when food is short, tapping energy reserves (body fat) at a slow rate. It is the animal's slowed metabolic rate which leads to a reduction in body temperature and not the other way around. Hibernation may last several days or weeks depending on species, ambient temperature, and time of year. The typical winter season for a hibernator is characterized by periods of hibernation interrupted by sporadic euthermic arousals wherein body temperature is restored to typical levels."

Hibernation is generally distinguished from torpor. "Torpor is usually short-term, and involves decreased physiological activity in an animal, typically a reduced body temperature and rate of metabolism." Some argue that torpor and hibernation are really the same, differing only in how long the animal is in the state of reduced activity. I will leave that argument to others.

The Hopi of the desert southwest know a bird which they call "holchko" - "the sleeping one." It is the Common Poorwill, a nightjar closely related to the Whip-poor-will and the Common Nighthawk. Nightjars are nondescript birds with large heads. They forage at night on the wing, their gaping mouths capturing insects as they fly. The Common Poorwill is the smallest nightjar. Its preferred habitat is dry, open grassland with a few bushes.

In 1946, Professor Edmund Jaeger was doing a routine survey in the Chuckwalla Mountains of California. In a crevice he found a Common Poorwill "sleeping peacefully through the cold winter. He returned to the location annually to find that the bird did likewise, using the same crevice year after year for its winter repose." The Hopi were right; "the sleeping one" was in hibernation, not precisely sleep but close enough.

It is now acknowledged that sometimes the Common Poorwill hibernates. Pete Dunne writes of its Movement/Migration: "More questions than answers here. Most or all northern birds apparently migrate to more temperate portions of the range ... In response to cold stress, this species hibernates, but how commonly or widely remains unknown."

Aristotle was right about birds hibernating. He just got the species wrong.

Hibernation by the Common Poorwill involves slowing its metabolism and dropping its body temperature, and maintaining that state for an extended length of time. In laboratory conditions, this state could be induced by depriving food. Comparable results were obtained with the Lesser Nighthawk, a similar species.

On cold winter nights in Vermont, how do our backyard chickadees manage to survive? One strategy would be to roost together in a tree cavity protected from the weather, and shiver through the night in order to maintain their body temperature of 105 degrees. That is an energy expensive survival tactic.

Studies have shown that chickadees, as well as roadrunners, swallows, and swifts, are able to lower their body temperature and become torpid. That is, they engage in an overnight, or short-term, hibernation in order to deal with the cold and save energy.

Studies of the Hillstar Hummingbird which lives in the Andes

Mountain above 12,500 feet show that it routinely engages in nocturnal hibernation. Hummingbirds need lots of energy for flight. They cannot feed at night. "So to stay alive, the hillstar seeks a safe roost in a cave, where it remains overnight in a state of torpor for seven to ten hours." It lowers its body temperature to 40 to 50 degrees. "At morning's first light, they rev up their metabolic motors to reheat and leave their refuge in search of nectar-bearing flowers."

My dear companion worries about the chickadees and titmice during bitter winter nights. But it may be that these small birds have a much more effective way of staying warm through such nights than we do. We stay warm by burning money (alright, it's really fuel oil, but a lot of it). They become torpid, saving energy by lowering their metabolism and body temperature and using almost no energy.

I suspect that a lot of birds engage in some sort of torpor or short-term hibernation when conditions call for it.

Bicknell's Thrush nests in high elevation boreal forests

CHAPTER 48

HOW BICKNELL GOT HIS OWN THRUSH

How did Bicknell get a thrush named for him? And who was Bicknell in the first place?

Eugene P. Bicknell (1859-1925) counted among his ancestors a knight who fought with William the Conqueror in 1066, early colonists who settled in Massachusetts and Rhode Island, one of the founders of Yale College, and an episcopal rector who remained loyal to the king during the American Revolution and was forced to flee to Canada. With such prominence in his background, he did not need a college degree to enter the New York banking world where he eventually became a partner in a prestigious foreign banking firm.

But none of this is why he became the possessor of his own thrush. Self educated and well educated, he was interested in natural history from a very young age. Today he would be called a birder and throughout his life he remained an amateur naturalist. Contemporaries knew him as an ornithologist. "The Auk," the journal of the American Ornithological Union, in 1926 remembered him as "one of the very few ornithologists of his time who habitually used the field glass more than the gun and kept daily lists of every species seen. His hearing in those days was especially acute and discriminating, so that he was often able to pick out a low, lisping note from a loud medley of bird song."

In 1878, at the age of nineteen, he published his first technical paper, "Evidences of the Carolinian Fauna in the Lower Hudson Valley." In the same year, he was one of the ten original organizers (and youngest) of the Linnaean Society of New York, sometimes called one of the aristocrats of American bird clubs. He was the club president from 1879 to 1887.The club still holds regular meetings at the American Museum of Natural History, offers regular lectures, field trips, and a rare bird alert.

In 1884 (now aged 25), Bicknell was one of the founders of the American Ornithological Union and was appointed to the committees on Migration of Birds and on The European House Sparrow, and soon after to the original committee on Bird Protection.

Bicknell's interests gradually turned toward botany and he wrote a number of important botanical papers. Later in his life, his interests returned to ornithology, He did careful studies of Long Island bird life whenever business gave him the freedom to do so. "He was skillful in the use of telescopes, carrying a 40-power for still subjects and using a 20-power for birds in flight, picking up and following flocks of wild fowl with ease as they sped along the coast. His ability to identify a live bird in the field often seemed remarkable." ("The Auk," April, 1926)

All this may be interesting, but it still does not explain how this banker and amateur naturalist got his own thrush. For that explanation we have to go to June 15, 1881, when 21 year old Eugene Bicknell hired a local guide and climbed Slide Mountain in the Catskills of New York.

"After a difficult hike through rain, cold and fog he arrived near the summit to parting skies. In a small opening in the fir forest Mr. Bicknell heard Swainson's Thrushes singing and calling. Then he heard an unfamiliar song that was more reminiscent of a Veery. A thrush-sized bird flew across the opening ...." Bicknell may have been unusual among the naturalists of his day in his use of field glasses, but on this occasion he used his shotgun to collect the thrush.

Young Bicknell startled the ornithological community. Just outside America's largest metropolitan area and in the backyard of many great ornithologists, he had found a new thrush. He sent his specimen to the American Museum of Natural History where the curator of ornithology studied it. The newly discovered bird was named Bicknell's Thrush in his honor, but it was classified scientifically as a subspecies of the Gray-cheeked Thrush. Bicknell's Thrush bore the binomial scientific name of the Gray-cheeked Thrush with the addition of a third name, *bicknelli*.

After the initial study, Bicknell's discovery languished. A cynic might think that the professionals in the bird community, with all of their learning and expertise, could not imagine that a young amateur had found something completely new which they had not found. Consequently, there was no need to study the new thrush further. That may not be fair, but the fact is, for fifty years Bicknell's Thrush was ignored by ornithologists.

In the 1930s, Bicknell's Thrush became the subject of a doctoral dissertation. The doctoral student found that Bicknell's Thrush was smaller than the Gray-cheeked Thrush, and had a stronger yellow color at the base of the lower bill. When the researcher examined specimens in hand, he could easily distinguish the two. However, he did not risk having his dissertation rejected by his learned examiners and recommended that Bicknell's Thrush remain a subspecies of the Gray-cheeked Thrush.

For another sixty years, Bicknell's Thrush continued to languish as a subspecies. In 1993, Dr. Henri Ouellet of the National Museum of Canada published his reexamination of the classification of Bicknell's Thrush. He confirmed that Bicknell's Thrush is smaller than the Gray-cheeked Thrush and has color variations. In addition, he found that summer and winter ranges did not overlap, that there were differences in the calls and songs, and that the birds did not appear to respond to the songs of the other.

Next, DNA studies were done by Dr. Gilles Seutin, another Canadian. "He found significant divergence between the two birds and estimated that they probably separated from a common ancestor about one million years ago."

And finally, in 1995 the American Ornithological Union examined all of the evidence. They accorded Bicknell's Thrush full species status: *Catharus bicknelli*.

Catharus derives from the Greek for "pure" - perhaps a reference to the "purity" with which the members of this genus sing. The Genus *Catharus* includes the Veery, Hermit Thrush, Gray-cheeked Thrush, and Swainson's Thrush.

The species name, *bicknelli*, honors, of course, Eugene Bicknell. 114 years after this amateur ornithologist, then only 21 years old, discovered this new thrush, the scientific community recognized the uniqueness of his discovery.

Of course, the story of Eugene Bicknell's Thrush is not over. The long neglect of Eugene Bicknell's new thrush is over; it is intensely studied (relatively speaking) in the Northeast by biologists of the Vermont Center for Ecostudies. Just in time. It's winter habitat in the Caribbean is threatened by the indiscriminate clearing of forests. It's breeding habitat on islands of boreal forest is threatened by acid raid, airborne pollutants, and climate warming and stressed by recreational development and use. So recently recognized as a species, the very survival of Bicknell's Thrush is in danger.

Common Raven

CHAPTER 49

RAVEN

Early this week, I was pursuing sparrows in the Retreat Meadows and watching jays mob a young Red-tailed Hawk perched in a cottonwood. Overhead, I heard "cur-ruk, cur-ruk." Raven flew steadily, his dark form heading steadily on a raven task.

Last week at Dead Creek in Addison, I watched a first year Bald Eagle hunting while a dozen crows harassed its every movement. Overhead, I heard "cur-ruk, cur-ruk," as Raven flew steadily, a few flaps and glide, unmoved by his cousins' distress over the eagle.

In mid-October, I had watched several ravens cavorting on the updraft currents, dipping and swirling and diving, and all the time talking: "Cur-ruk." "Kraak." "Cronk, cur-ruk."

One dark night at home, I pulled an old and worn volume off the shelf and turned the frayed pages:

" ... I betook myself to linking

216

Fancy unto fancy, thinking what this ominous bird of yore –

What this grim, ungainly, ghastly, gaunt, and ominous bird of yore

Meant in croaking, 'Nevermore.'"

The tormented, troubled mind of Edgar Allan Poe turned to the raven for the embodiment of darkness, depression, and death as he struggled with his inconsolable sorrow for the lost Lenore. His deliriums and tremens found expression in the "The Raven," and has locked the symbolism of this great black bird on the side of night in popular western literature.

This dark side of Raven has a long history. Ravens are opportunistic omnivores, quite content to dine on carrion. Coming out of the dark forests onto an ancient battlefield, they appeared to relish the carnage. The fearsome Celtic warrior goddess, Morrigan, was served by ravens. She was capable of turning the tide in war. She could turn herself into a raven to survey the battlefield and encourage her chosen side to new levels of brutality. When the battle was over, and ravens descended to the battlefield, she would feast with them on the bodies of the dead.

It is hardly surprising that the reputation of the raven was often a grim one, associated with sorrow and death, with the devil and darkness. In some areas of England, hats are tipped to ravens in order not to offend them and children are told that the Great Black Bird will carry them off if they are bad.

Poor, mad E.A.Poe took himself so seriously that he could only take Raven seriously as well. Too bad for Poe. With better powers of observation and less brooding introspection, peoples across the northern hemisphere, from tundra to desert, coast to mountain, in North America, Europe, and Asia, have also seen a different side to Raven and have celebrated Raven's native intelligence.

Raven is a royal bird. Alexander the Great was guided across the desert by two ravens sent from heaven. King Arthur was turned into a raven. For over 900 years, ravens have lived in the Tower of London. It is said that if the ravens ever leave the Tower of London, the Tower will fall, and if the Tower falls, the Crown of England to which it is tied will fall - and if the Crown falls, then England will fall. The ravens have never left the Tower of London; clipped wings may have aided in their loyal defense of the Crown.

Modern bird guides are pretty straightforward when they report the habits of birds, seldom anthropomorphizing bird behavior. But even sober Cornell Lab of Ornithology cannot refrain from reporting that ravens "engage in seemingly playful acts. They are known to yank the tails of cats and dogs and even to peck on their victim's noses."

Sibley's *Bird Life and Behavior* reports on their intelligence and problem solving ability. "Ravens faced with a novel task, such as getting food that is dangling on the end of a string, were able to assess the problem and then use their feet to hold the string and pull the food up. They performed this action without missteps the first time they attempted it."

This innate intelligence inspired the folklore and mythology of diverse peoples in the Northern Hemisphere, no more so than among the Native Americans of the Pacific Northwest. There Raven is a special totem, considered by many to be the creator of humankind. He brought them salmon to eat. He stole fire from the sun so humans would not freeze. He brought them water during a drought. He taught people to enjoy life.

In the Pacific Northwest, Raven is life giving, a helping and nurturing spirit. There is self-sacrifice in his actions; he does what he does to ensure the happiness of others. Raven is associated with joy and laughter. He is the Trickster, but his tricks are usually beneficial ones, teaching people to laugh at their own follies. Raven is the great magician, able to change shape and bring change to peoples lives. He also sees through the lies and tricks of others. Raven is curious, a gatherer of information and a sharer of secrets. Raven is a searcher for truth. Raven is a contradiction. He is black and white, joy and sorrow, savior and nemesis.

Half a world away from the Native Americans of the Pacific Northwest, the Norsemen of Scandinavia honored Odin, chief god in the mythology of the Eddas, god of war, of wisdom, and of poetry. Odin was attended by two ravens named Hugin, "thought," and Munin, "memory." Their job was to keep him informed of everything that happened on the earth. When Hugin and Munin, the two ravens, left him, Odin was without thought or memory until they returned. Then they would tell him stories of all they had witnessed or heard. Because of Odin's affinity with these birds, the Norse revered all ravens and still tell stories about these birds.

Poe's raven spoke but a single word, a word of finality and despair: "Nevermore." But Raven has returned to the mountains and hills of the East after a hundred year absence. "Cur-ruk, cur-ruk, cur-ruk," calls Raven along the ridges and over the hills. I think he saying, "Evermore!"

The Vermont Brigade

In these woods during the Battle of the Wilderness on May 5 and 6, 1864, Vermont's "Old Brigade" suffered 1,234 casualties while defending the Brock Road and Orange Plank Road intersection.

CHAPTER 50

WHEN THE BIRDS WERE SILENT

A mockingbird sang from the top of a cherry tree in full bloom. From a bush beneath the trees, a yellowthroat claimed his realm with "witchety, witchety, witchety." More distantly, a towhee, just beginning to search for a territory, called "chewink."

We looked across the open fields - a dip in front of us - then a gentle rise. The grasses were just greening up from the new warmth of the spring sun. We followed a mown pathway through the field toward the rise. A lone tree stood near the crest. Somewhere among its branches, a Chipping Sparrow trilled forth his notes.

From the crest of the "ridge," we looked down the other side of the gentle slope toward the edge of the woods. Somewhere within the forest cover, a Wood Thrush played his flute: "Eee-Oh-Lay." Back among the grasses, a Field Sparrow sang, his song, a series of plaintive notes speeding up as he sang, something like a ping pong ball whose "pings" become faster as gravity takes hold. It was peaceful, pastoral - a misty, gray Spring day filled with song and full of the promise of life.

And yet, there was a deep disconnect as we stood on the grassy rise, a melancholy which no birdsong could assuage. On this day, we were not birding. We were tracing the movement of thousands of men in the Spring of 1864. The peaceful fields we were standing in are part of the Spotsylvania National Military Park where the armies of Grant and Lee, the North and the South, clashed in some of the most horrible and bloody fighting of our fratricidal Civil War.

Earlier in the morning, we had followed the beginning of the days long battles. For convenience, historians call the first clash the Battle of the Wilderness. Land with no use to farmers had been clear logged, then abandoned to regrow as it might. Small trees, thick brush, and tangled brambles rendered it a nearly impenetrable "wilderness."

A critical spot in this battle was the intersection of Brock Road and Orange Plank Road. A young forest lines these roads today. We walked a wide, cushioned path through the woods. The fighting those years ago had been so intense that the thick wilderness growth had been thinned and shorn by musket balls. Now it was thinned by the natural growth and succession of the forest. At the end of the path stood a simple, granite monument. Put in place just last year, the monument commemorates the Vermont Brigade.

Considered by many historians to be one of the two or three finest brigades in the northern armies, the Vermonters were told to hold the intersection at all costs. They did, and at a frightful cost - over a thousand killed, wounded, and missing. We stood quietly reading the simple inscription which could not mask the valor, or the horror, of this place. The woods about us were silent. Traffic noise was distant. No song broke the silence; even the birds were silent.

We resumed our "tour." Not far from the once bloody intersection, was a monumental entrance way to a gated community. The super-sized mansions beyond were protected from prying eyes. That so many had died on those grounds was irrelevant next to developmental profits, and conspicuous exclusivity.

The Battle of the Wilderness was a stand-off. The armies maneuvered a few miles down the road. Lee's army dug their trenches for miles around Spotsylvania Court House and Grant dug in around Lee's lines. A park road follows many of those trenches with numerous pull-outs and interpretive signs. Many of those signs are old and weather-worn, often difficult to read. They stand as monuments to current national values - billions for today's war - pittance for the lessons of history and the heritage of the nation.

Driving through a stretch of open field, a murder of crows took flight. There were a couple dozen of the big black birds - probably second or third year birds still learning their way, discovering whether they could find enough to feed themselves before pairing and nesting. Over the field, a Turkey Vulture drifted in lazy circles. At the end of the road we parked, and walked across the field.

And so we stood on that ridge. From the woods, Union troops moved unseen to the crest of the ridge, then stormed down and up toward the trenches of the Confederate troops. This was the "Bloody Angle" where a day in early May would bring twenty continuous hours of vicious and desperate combat, often hand to hand - where a twenty-two inch tree was cut down by musket fire - where even the bloodied and thinned ranks of the Vermont Brigade would again be thrust into the slaughter.

The Chipping Sparrow sang, not for us, but for a mate to continue life. So did the Field Sparrow, and the towhee, and the mockingbird, and the thrush. But on that day in May, 1864, I have no doubt that the birds were silent. That cannon fire, and musketry, and the screams of dying men did not just overwhelm the Spring songs, but drove them from the field in horrified silence.

Some 140,000 men participated in these battles. Combined casualties were thirty percent. Spotsylvania, like the Wilderness, was a stand-off. Once again the armies moved, southward to defend or attack the Confederate capital in Richmond. So quickly did they abandon these battlefields that the dead remained where they had fallen.

It was a year before teams returned to these killing fields to find and bury the dead. But I have no doubt that the fallen were attended to. It would have been a boon year for the scavengers. They would eat heartily and their young would thrive. Turkey Vultures who need only a few airborne molecules to locate carrion would have gathered from hundreds of miles around. Smaller birds needing the protein of insects, grubs, and maggots would have easy foraging. By Fall, the murder of young crows would have mushroomed. It is a horror vision to evoke in our sanitized modern world - that nature would be so cavalier and callous toward a fallen soldier. But even in our filtered environment, we are not free from the cavalier and callous. Those adjectives, cavalier and callous, are rightly applied to many human animals - to our species which apparently possesses self-awareness and claims to have a moral sensitivity.

The birds were silent on that day in May of 1864. As we looked toward the old trenches where men clashed so violently and fatally, the songs seemed muted. But it was not the birds which stirred my thoughts. It was the horror of events, past and present. And I wondered, what difference might it make today if those who vote for war must also fight in war? - Or at the least, send their own daughters and sons to fight in the wars they make?

Clark's Nutcracker, a Corvid, is about to snatch, and cache, human food

CHAPTER 51

WISE GUYS AND THIEVES

Human beings can be arrogant. And immediately, many readers may wonder why I would begin with such a trivial and obvious statement. We have many thing about which we are arrogant; the particular arrogance I have in mind is the one that considers human beings to be the only creature on the planet capable of thinking, and reasoning, and solving problems. There are human beings, and there are all of the other dumb creatures.

Our vast intelligence makes some of us curious. A few of those who are curious begin to wonder about things which they see. They see things among the dumb creatures that suggest there is more intelligence among those dumb creatures than we have been willing to admit. Now we all know that our family pet is smart. It knows when it is going for a walk (you took out the leash). It knows when it is going to the kennel (you are packing a suitcase). It know when you are going to give it a special dinner treat (you are cutting up the scraps on your dinner plate). But that doesn't really count, because the family pet is just a furry little human being. And it lives inside the house. Creatures which live outside are still, basically, dumb, living by instinct.

Well maybe not. A few curious researchers have been testing the dumb creature hypothesis, and over and over they are finding that maybe the dumb creatures are not quite so dumb after all.

Let's take for example, the *Corvidae* - the family of the crows, jays, and magpies. The family in general, and the Genus *Corvus* in particular (crows and ravens) has been recognized as one of the most intelligent in the bird world. Our ancient ancestors, who were acute observers of the natural world, recognized the Corvids as unique, and wove them through their legends and myths. Ravens were the eyes and ears of the Norse god, Odin. Raven was the trickster in dozens of North American mythologies - at once benevolent and capricious, a boon and a bane, the playful prankster and the malevolent source of evil.

The rich mythologies disappeared before the onslaught of theologies touting the crown of creation - humans. Then came the age of reason, and the reasoning of science. And the eyes and ears of Odin became mechanistic creatures acting on instinct, but with no will and no mind.

Let's take another look at the raven. When a raven pair has finished raising their young, they continue to live in, and defend, their nesting territory, while sending their young off into the world. Young ravens gather in flocks, sometimes quite large, and wander widely. In these flocks, they may eventually find a mate. They cooperate in finding food - often carcasses. A hierarchy also develops in the flock. It is not clear what gives one bird a higher rank than another, but it is clear that there is an established "pecking" order. The dominant bird feeds first; the subservient bird waits.

There is cooperation in finding food, but it does not follow that there is a willingness to share food. Bernd Heinrich, in his study of winter ravens, discovered that the dominant bird not only feeds first and to its fill, but goes beyond that. It takes food and stashes it - hides it some distance off. A subservient raven, kept from feeding on the carcass by higher ranked birds, carefully watched the food being carried off and hidden. As soon as it could, it stole the food cached by the dominant raven.

The raven who cached its extra food, discovered the theft. Knowing it was being watched, this raven then pretended to hide food in its cache. It went through an elaborate hiding ritual, then took its food to a new, and it hoped, now secret location. This is not the behavior of dumb, mechanistic creatures.

This raven behavior was studied in the frigid, winter woods of Maine. Occasionally, observers can put two and two together, even in a busy city, and come up with four. A television crew in a Japanese city filmed some crows. The urban crows were fond of the meat of a particular nut. But they do not have the ability to crack open the nut. So they drop the nut on a city street and wait for it to be run over by automobiles. But the roads are busy, and cars are dangerous. How safely to get the tasty meat from the cracked nut?

They found a solution. They perch on a wire above a pedestrian crosswalk, and drop the nut. Traffic runs over the nut and cracks it open. Then when the light changes and the cars stop, they fly down to the crosswalk when they only have to avoid the pedestrians and scarf down the cracked nut. Not such nutty behavior.

So apparently the corvids can do some thinking, some planning ahead, and some problem solving. They can also, hoard, not share, and commit crime. Instead of being dumb mechanistic creatures, they have a lot of human characteristics. Darn!

The corvids aren't the only wise guys and thieves out there. If you've ever been to the beach, you have probably seen similar behavior among the gulls. Maybe you've seen one try to break open a mollusk by dropping it on a rocky shelf or a paved road. They are also quite content to steal food from other gulls, or anyone or anything else. I once had one beg insistently from me. I finally threw it a piece of cucumber from my sandwich. It liked the cucumber so much, it stole the rest of the sandwich when I wasn't looking. Now, which creature was dumb and outsmarted?

And then there is the Herring Gull in England that developed an inordinate fondness for cheese Doritos. Every day it walked through the open door of a small convenience store, grabbed a bag of cheese Doritos (only that kind) and walked out - without paying. Outside, it tore open the bag and ate the contents. Apparently there is not enough crime in that English city to fill the evening news, so a television crew caught the thieving gull on film in the very act of its crime.

What am I going to make of all this? That some birds are smarter than we think? That most humans are dumber than we think? That with brains comes crime? Probably all true.

I think I will suggest that a bit more humility about our place in the scheme of things is the most appropriate response. I have been reading theology much longer than I have been watching birds. I have long been struck by theologies which tout the magnificent, majesty, omnipotence and omniscience of the Creator. I have been equally struck that most of those theologies are absolutely certain that they know the mind and will of the Creator. That seems like a striking contradiction. If the first is true, as I am willing to concede, then the response should be one of deep and profound humility, not an arrogance which presumes to know and speak in behalf of the divine.

When I see the wise guys and thieves among the crows and ravens and gulls, they lead me to the conclusion that we humans need something unique in order to claim a place of primacy in creation - like compassion, goodwill, generosity. In the meantime - and even then - humility is in order.

Maybe a first step is to find some ways that we can tread more lightly and live more gently. Maybe that will begin to give some of the other creatures a chance to figure out how to make their way on this planet that we have so altered.

CHAPTER 52

THE BIG DAY'S "BEST BIRD"

Near the end of our "Big Day," our annual 24 hour self-contest to see how many birds we can identify in Windham County, we took a break. We (being myself, Richard and Eric) drove from Herrick's Cove to Chester where David Sibley of the highly acclaimed Sibley bird guides was speaking.

During the course of his engaging, unassuming talk, Sibley described what it is that draws him to bird watching; it is the allure of not knowing what is out there, the sense of anticipation, and the process of discovering what is there, what is unexpected, and sometimes what is missing.

It is that very allure that had us driving around the County in search of birds. By mid-afternoon, we were astounded at some of the birds we had missed: Tufted Titmouse, Rose-breasted Grosbeak, and Belted Kingfisher we had considered as definite. The first two were daily fixtures at our feeders, while the kingfisher can be heard along every river, stream, lake and pond. At the end of the day, they remained unticked. (The next day, each of us saw or heard all three in different locations - such are the vagaries of birding.)

We had considered the American Kestrel as a probable, in spite its steadily declining numbers. But every prime kestrel habitat we visited, every kestrel box we put our binoculars on, every farm stead and power line where they have often been seen, was bereft of this small falcon.

We were less worried about the Great Blue Heron. Although we had been in many beaver ponds, marshes, river and stream sides, by early evening we had still not seen the heron. But our last daylight stop was Herrick's Cove, and we were quite confident that the Great Blue would be there. And this time our confidence was not misplaced. Our first scan of the cove produced several herons wading in the shallow water. Still, we would hardly have anticipated that this large, prominent bird would be number 100 for the day.

We were studying a small flock of gulls, hoping that one of the Ring-billed Gulls might be something different. No such luck. But with binoculars to our eyes, a male kestrel flew across our field of view. Following the kestrel, we saw swallows scattering. A small flock of Least Sandpipers (an unexpected sighting) burst into panicked flight. In one of the least likely habitats, we finally ticked the kestrel and broke the one hundred mark.

The water in Herrick's cove was very low, making it difficult to negotiate the canoe among the islands in the hopes of hearing a Sora or Virginia Rail. But the exposed mudflats produced a Greater Yellowlegs, and (totally unexpected) a couple of Black-bellied Plovers and a dozen Semipalmated Plovers.

Earlier that day in the mid-morning, we were working our way along Forest Route 71 through Somerset. Sometimes there is something that tells you to stop and get out of your vehicle. We did that. A Canada Warbler greeted us with his song. A little bit of "phishing" brought him into view, and we saw the plain gray back, yellow neck and breast, and the black "necklace" that distinguishes this bird of the undergrowth and mid forest levels.

Through small openings in the trees, we could see the extensive wetlands of a beaver pond. In a patch of open water were several male Wood Ducks. They have only one function in the perpetuation of their species, and having performed that function, they leave parenthood to the females and gather with other males for a Wood Duck stag party.

Then with restrained glee I said to the others, "Check out the moose."

We worked our way through the undergrowth to get closer to the edge of the interconnected ponds. The bull moose went about feeding, unconcerned about our none-too-subtle approached through the tangle of trees and shrubs, over trickling rills and humps of grass. The cow kept an eye on us. A third moose, another bull, eventually ambled off into the woods, although I'm not sure you can describe anything that a moose does as ambling.

The three moose did not completely distract us from our birding. A Northern Waterthrush was singing at some distance. Swamp Sparrows were closer at hand; their song is much like that of a Chipping Sparrow. The subtle differences in the songs of these two sparrows may be confounding - they also look quite similar - but habitat is a certain clue. My crude rule of thumb is that a Chippy singing in a swamp is a Swamp Sparrow.

While the wet ground sucked our rubber boots into its grip, we also ticked off Tree Swallow, Red-winged Blackbird, Common Grackle, Chimney Swift, and Mallard. All of these are common birds which have adapted to the presence of humans and the habitat changes which our presence has created on the landscape. The Chimney Swift, for example, is named because it nests in chimneys, an adaptation to environmental change caused by the clearing of the land and the removal of the large hollow trees in which it used to nest.

Each of these familiar birds seemed more at home, more natural in a setting created by the beaver, rather than one created or heavily altered by humans. I know that there are all kinds of logical inconsistencies and romantic notions in such a notion, but that's all right. There are times when I need to feel as though I am connected with a past time, or an untouched natural order. It puts me in my place. I am a piece of the creation, which lives best when living in touch, in harmony, or just in association, with the infinite variations of life itself.

The allure of not knowing what's out there, the sense of anticipation, the excitement of discovery - that's why I go birding - that's why I do a "Big Day." So, of the 108 birds we saw that day, what was the best bird?

Without a doubt, the three moose!

Chapter Notes

3. Ravensnest

Audubon quotation from John James Audubon, *The Birds of America*, Dover edition, 1967, Vol. 4, p.82.

Bent's *Life History* quotation from Arthur Cleveland Bent, *Life Histories of North American Jays, Crows and Titmice* first published 1946. Dover edition 1964, Part One, p. 198f.

5. Those Wonderful Wood Warblers

Bird song mnemonics are tools which try to express on paper complex bird songs. The only precision in these mnemonics is how well they may help a birder who is learning birds songs to remember, or to enable a writer to convey something of the music and language of birds. The Chestnut-sided Warbler is a case in point. In this chapter I rendered the song in three different ways; each is partly the result of my listening to this bird sing and partly the result of reading and processing various field guides as they try to describe a song. Here is the rendering of several guides:

Kaufman - sweet, sweet, sweet, seesaWEETchew
National Geographic - please, please, please, pleased to meetcha
Peterson - see see see see Miss BEECHer
    or please please pleased to MEETcha
Sibley - witew witew witew WEECHEW
Dunne - S'swee S'swee S'swee z'WEECHU
    rendered Please Please Please to MEET YOU
Stokes - pleased, pleased, pleased to meet ya
Walton & Lawson - please please please to meet'cha

Mnemonics are used so frequently and so matter-of-factly by birders, and in so many variations, that they have become an integral component in the culture of bird watching.

8. Backyard Peyton Place

Forbush quotation summarizes a report from Mr. S. Prentisss

Baldwin. Edward Howe Forbush, *Birds of Massachusetts and Other New England States, 1929*, Vol. 3, p.343.

Sibley quotations are from "Reproductive Behavior" by Cech, Dunning, and Elphick in *The Sibley Guide to Bird Life and Behavior*, 2001, page 71f.

12. Birding in the Town of Stratton

Kaufman quotation from *Birds of North America*, 2000, p. 278.

17. Black Scoter Visits Newfane

Dunne quotation from *Pete Dunne's Essential Field Guide Companion*, 2006, p. 58.

Forbush quotation from Edward Howe Forbush and John Bichard May, *A Natural History of American Birds of Eastern and Central North America*, 1955, p. 87f.

18. Hawk Folk Names

Forbush & May, *American Birds* ...., lists "Other names" for the species they describe, and these were the starting point for this essay. Forbush often went to great lengths to demonstrate the "economic" benefit of birds. In relation to the predators, he downplayed or tried to disprove their supposed danger to domestic fowl.

20. Kinglet Versus Winter's Worst

Heinrich quotation from Bernd Heinrich, *Winter World, The Ingenuity of Animal Survival*, 2003, p.128-129.

21. Vermont's Elusive Bicknell's Thrush

Dunne quotation, *Pete Dunne's Essential Field Guide Companion*, 2006, p. 499.

25. Sex in Winter

Forbush quotation from Edward Howe Forbush and John Bichard May, *A Natural History of American Birds of Eastern and Central North America*, 1955 ,p. 77.

35. Bobolink

The website of the Vermont Center for Ecostudies contains an excellent summary of Dr. Renfrew's research: www.vtecostudies.org - under the link, Wildlife Research.

Forbush quotation from Edward Howe Forbush and John Bichard May, *A Natural History of American Birds of Eastern and Central North America*, 1955, p. 459.

39. Shotgun Ornithology

Weidensaul quotation from Scott Weidensaul, *Of a Feather*, 2007, p.142

A reference in this essay and elsewhere for the origin of bird names is Ernest A. Choate, *American Bird Names, 1985.*

Dunne quotation from *Pete Dunne's Essential Field Guide Companion*, 2006, p. 457.

41. Common Raven

Heinrich quotation from Bernd Heinrich, *Ravens in Winter*, 1987, p. 313.

42. Tough City Birds

Examining, and sometimes deflating, conventional wisdom has always attracted me. There is conventional wisdom toward the city (a wildlife desert) and the few birds that thrive in the city (pigeon). The article in Sierra, "Sex and the City Bird, March/April, 2008, was a very short article, but it made me reconsider a few bits of conventional wisdom.

47. Aristotle

The remarkable migration of birds can be found in many books dealing with the subject.

Much of the historical framework for this chapter was assisted by Janice M. Hughes, *The Migration of Birds*, 2009, which tells the fascinating history and science of migration. It is a glossy, small-sized coffee table book that merits a thorough reading. Hughes is quoted regarding Hillstar Hummingbird and Common Poorwill, p. 32, regarding Blackpoll Warbler, p. 121. She quotes Coues on p.32.

Definitions of "hibernation" and "torpor" are from Wikipedia:
en.wikipedia.org/wiki/Hibernation
en.wikipedia.org/wiki/Torpor

Dunne quotation from *Pete Dunne's Essential Field Guide Companion*, 2006, p.347.

48. How Bicknell Got His Own Thrush
Environment Canada has a website on Bicknell's Thrush which provided much of the background for this column:
   www.atl.ec.gc.ca/wildlife/bicknells_thrush/e/index.html
   Except for the quotation from *The Auk*, the quotations are from this website.

49. Raven
   As one with an appreciation for the work of the academic researcher, I shudder at the thought that many students today consider a google search to constitute research. Nevertheless, there is a wealth of information available through today's search engines. Without a good academic library nearby, I have relied often on Google to lead me in my search for background on what I write about, in this instance, the rich lore of the Raven,
   Sibley quotation from Elphick, et al., *The Sibley Guide to Bird Life and Behavior,* 2001, p.412.

51. Wise Guys and Thieves
   The reader who may have his/her interest peaked by my fascination with ravens should read Bernd Heinrich, *Ravens in Winter*, 1989, and *Mind of the Raven*, 1999.
   Videos of the nutcracking crows and the Dorito stealing gull can be seen on Bird Cinema:

Selected Resources

The resources and literature on birds for the casual hobbyist and the serious birder has exploded. These "Selected Resources" are the places I turn most often for identification help, background, information, science, and entertainment as I pursue my hobbies of bird watching, bird photography, and writing about birds.

Field Guides

No one field guide is the perfect guide. Every guide has strengths and weaknesses. For difficult identifications, it will be necessary to compare several guides. Among the many excellent general field guides, these are the ones which I use most often, and I recommend that new birders begin with one or more of these.

•Dun, Jon L. and Jonathan Alderfer, *National Geographic Field Guide to the Birds of North America*, 5th edition, 2006

•Kaufman, Kenn, *Birds of North America*, 2000.

•Peterson, Roger Tory. *Field Guide to the Birds* of North America, 2008.

   A Field Guide to the Birds of Eastern and Central North America, 5th edition, 2002.

   A Field Guide to Western Birds, 4th edition, 2009.

•Sibley, David Allen, *The Sibley Guide to Birds*, 2000.

   The Sibley Field Guide to Birds of Western North America, 2003.

   The Sibley Field Guide to Birds of Eastern North America, 2003.

•Stokes, Donald & Lillian, *The Stokes Field Guide to the Birds of North America*, 2010

Electronic Field Guides

•Mitch Waite Group*, iBird Explorer Pro,* 2006-2010.

•Sibley, David Allen, *The Sibley eGuide to the Birds of North America*, 2003-2010.

Bird Songs

•Kroodsma, Donald, *The Backyard Birdsong Guide, a Guide to Listening*, 2008.

•*Stokes Field Guide to Bird Songs, Eastern Region*, 3CDs, 1997.
  Western Region, 4CDs, 1999.

These two Stokes collections are the most complete collections for North America. Each comes with a booklet to find the tracks. If you are only using the CDs, finding the track of a particular bird is cumbersome. However, *birdJam Maker* (www.birdjam.com) is an iPod application which organizes the bird songs into playlists and makes it possible to find and listen to a particular bird in about 30 seconds. It is very useful in the field. Most electronic field guides also include bird songs, though not as many variations as contained in the Stokes collections.

•Walton, Ruchard K. & Robert W. Lawson, *Birding by Ear, A Guide to Bird Song Identification*, 1989.
  More Birding by Ear, 1994.

These are teaching guides, and they are excellent. I used the early cassette editions to learn basic bird songs. Excellent tool to get started.

International

•Mullarney, Killian, et al., *Birds of Europe,* 1999. ... well, because, you just never know what might be where ...

Specialty Guides

There are many guides which focus on particular types of birds. Shorebirds, gulls, and hawks are among the most challenging. I often encounter the limitations of the general field guides and turn to one of the specialty guides.

Gulls

•Grant, P.J., Gulls, *A Guide to Identification,* 1999.

•Olsen, Klaus Malling & Hans Larsson, *Gulls of North America, Europe, and Asia*, 2004.

Hawks

•Clark, William S. & Brian K. Wheeler, *Hawks of North America*, 2nd edition, 2001.

•Dunne, Pete, David Sibley & Clay Sutton, *Hawks in Flight*, 1988.

•Wheeler, Brian K. & William S. Clark, *A Photographic Guide to North American Raptors,* 1995.

•Liguori, Jerry, *Hawks from Every Angle*, 2005.
•Wheeler, Brian K., *Raptors of Eastern North America*, 2003.
Other
•Early, Chris G., *Waterfowl of Eastern North America*, 2005.
•Jaramilla, Alvaro, and Peter Burke, *New World Blackbirds, The Icterids*, 1999.
•Madge, Steve, and Hilary Burn, *Crows & Jays*, 1994.
Shorebirds
•Chandler, Richard, *Shorebirds of North American, Europe, and Asia,* 2009
•Message, Stephen & Don Taylor, *Shorebirds of North America, Europe, and Asia. A Guide to Field Identification,* 2005.
•O'Brien, Michael, et al., *The Shorebird Guide,* 2006.

To Learn More About the Birds
•Audubon, John James, *The Birds of America,* 7 volumes. Dover edition replication, 1967, of octavo edition published in1871.
•Bent, Arthur Cleveland. *Life Histories of North American Birds,* 21 volumes, 1919-1968. Dover edition replication published 1964 & 1968.
•Choate, Ernest A., *American Bird Names,* 1985.
•Dunne, Pete, *Essential Field Guide Companion, A Comprehensive Resource for Identifying North American Birds,* 2006.
•Elphick, Chris, et al., *The Sibley Guide to Bird Life and Behavior,* 2001.
•Ehrlich, Paul R., et al., *The Birder's Handbook,* 1988.
•Forbush, Edward Howe, *Birds of Massachusetts and Other New England States*, 3 volumes, 1929.
•Forbush, Edward Howe & John Bichard May, *A Natural History of American Birds of Eastern and Central North America,* 1955. Essentially a one volume abridgement of the previous 3 volume work.
•Hughes, Janice M., *The Migration of Birds,* 2009.
•Kaufman, Kenn, *Lives of North American Birds,* 1996.
•Kroodsma, Donald, *The Singing Life of Birds, The Art and Science of Listening to Birdsong*, 2005.
•Leahy, Christopher W., *The Birdwatcher's Companion to North American Birdlife,* 2004.
•Lockwood, W.B., *The Oxford Book of British Bird Names,* 1984.
•Terres, John K., ed., *The Audubon Society Encyclopedia of North*

American Birds, 1980.
•Weidensaul, Scott, *The Raptor Almanac*, 2000.

Favorite Books & Authors
•Heinrich, Bernd. The nature writings of this University of Vermont biologist are exceptionally readable and engaging, and scientifically sound.
•Dunne, Pete. Any of the collected short essays by this "bard of birding."
•Kaufman, Kenn, *Kingbird Highway,* 1997.
•Rhodes, Richard, *John James Audubon: The Making of an American,* 2004.
•Rosenthal, Elizabeth J., *Birdwatcher, The Life of Roger Tory Peterson,* 2008.
•Weidensaul, Scott, *Living on the Wind, Across the Hemisphere with Migratory Birds*, 1999.
•Weidensaul, Scott, *Of a Feather, A Brief History of American Birding,* 2007.

Birding Basics
•Alderfer, Jonathan and Jon L. Dun, *National Geographic Birding Essentials*, 2007.
•Dunne, Pete. *Pete Dunne on Bird Watching,* 2003.
•Sibley, David Allen, *Sibley's Birding Basics,* 2002.

Where the Birds Are
There are many excellent guides on where to find birds. The American Birding Association publishes *A Birder's Guide...* for many of North America's best birding locales. The usefulness and usability of these guides is consistently good. There are also many state and regional guides from other organizations and publishers.

In Vermont, you will want:
•Murin, Ted & Bryan Pfeiffer, *Birdwatching in Vermont*, 2002.

With the growth in birding tourism, there are also many "birding trails" that have been developed, often with excellent brochures complete with good directions, best seasons, and other clues for finding birds.

www.ingramcontent.com/pod-product-compliance
Lightning Source LLC
Chambersburg PA
CBHW060243290526
45789CB00001B/168